Memories
of
Macclesfield

TRUE NORTH BOOKS

UNITS 3,4 & 5 HEATHFIELD INDUSTRIAL ESTATE
ELLAND, HALIFAX
WEST YORKSHIRE
HX5 9AE
TELEPHONE 01422 377977
FAX 01422 377677

THE PUBLISHERS WOULD LIKE TO THANK THE
FOLLOWING COMPANIES FOR SUPPORTING THE
PRODUCTION OF THIS BOOK

MAIN SPONSOR

ARIGHI BIANCHI

BAXTER, WOODHOUSE & TAYLOR LIMITED

ER BURGESS LIMITED

GORTON & WILSON (BUILDERS) LIMITED

SLATER HARRISON & COMPANY LIMITED

THE STORMGUARD GROUP

VACUUM FORMERS LIMITED

First published in Great Britain by True North Books
Elland
Halifax HX5 9AE
1999

© TRUE NORTH HOLDINGS
ISBN 1 900463 28 8

Introduction

Welcome to *Memories of Macclesfield*, a look back on some of the places, events and people in the town which have shaped the lives of local people over a period of around half a century. The following pages are brought to life by a selection of images from the not-too-distant past, chosen according to their ability to rekindle fond memories of days gone by and show how people used to shop, work and play in the area where they grew up. Modern image reproduction techniques have enabled us to present these pictures in a way rarely seen before, and the lively design and informative text has attempted to set the book apart from some of the other works available.

Macclesfield Market in the 1950s

The chosen period is one which generally contains events within the memory of a large number of people in Macclesfield - this is not a book about crinolines or bowler-hats! Neither is *Memories of Macclesfield* a work of local history in the normal sense of the term. It has far more to do with entertainment than serious study, but we hope you will agree it is none the worse for that. It is hoped that the following pages will prompt readers' own memories of Macclesfield from days gone by - and we are always delighted to hear from people who can add to the information contained in the captions so that we can enhance future editions of the book.

Local companies and organisations have allowed us to study their archives and include their history - and fascinating reading it makes too. The present-day guardians of the firms concerned are proud of their products, the achievements of their people and the hard work of their forefathers whose efforts created these long established organisations in the first place. We are pleased to play our part by making it possible for them to share their history with a wider audience.

When we began compiling *Memories of Macclesfield* several months ago we anticipated that the task would be a pleasurable one, but our expectations were greatly surpassed. There is a growing appetite for all things 'nostalgic' and we are pleased to have played a small part in swelling the number of images and associated information available to the growing number of enthusiasts.

There is much talk in modern times about the regeneration of the local economy, the influx of new industries and the challenge of attracting new enterprise from other regions to Macclesfield. And quite right too. We could, however, make the mistake of thinking that the changes are all happening *now*, but the reality is that there have always been major developments going on in the town. 'Change' is relentless and the photographs on the pages in the book serve to remind us of some of them.

Memories of Macclesfield has been a pleasure to compile, we sincerely hope you enjoy reading it.

Happy memories!

Text	*Peggy Burns*
Text pages design	*Mandy Walker and Nicky Brighton*
Photographs compiled by	*Mark Smith*
Business development	*Alan Eastham*
Copywriter	*Margaret Wakefield*

CONTENTS

Events & occasions

It was a sad time for the members of St Alban's Roman Catholic church when their priest, the well-loved Canon Cleary, died in 1937. Many saddened members of the congregation turned out to pay their respects, even bringing their children with them to say a last goodbye to the father who would be sadly missed. The funeral cortege is seen passing along Chester Road past St Alban's and the presbytery.

St Alban's church, designed by A W N Pugin, was built between 1839 and 1841, only the second RC church to be opened in Macclesfield since the Reformation. It was during the 19th century that many churches and chapels were opened in the

town. Roman Catholics, Anglicans, Baptists, Methodists, United Reform and even the Spiritualists opened churches in the mid to late 1800s. A major reason for this was of course that the town had increased in population during the reign of Queen Victoria. A second reason was the sovereign and her husband Prince Albert's firm stand on the importance of religion, moral standards, and family life.

It is interesting to note, however, that at the same time as the increase in the number of churches came a decided increase in the number of public houses being opened. In 1840 more than 200 pubs were licensed.

Above: Like a royal bride leaving the church after her wedding, the Silk Queen leaves the impressive pillared portico of the Infirmary to descend the stairway and join the grand carnival parade. This young lady would most likely be the retiring Silk Queen; a new queen would be chosen to replace her later in the day. Note the exquisite gowns of the silk princesses who lined up on the steps; every one was made from silk produced in Macclesfield. This is one photograph which begs a colour image. What colour were all those marvellous dresses? And the gorgeous flowers in the princesses' huge bouquets? The photograph probably dates from around 1933, and those marvellous small-brimmed hats worn by the ladies looking on are typical of the day's fashion.

The carnival was the occasion of the year and a red letter day in the town's diary. Probably headed up by the retiring Silk Queen, the decorated floats, the bands and the marchers would make their way through the streets of Macclesfield and into South Park. Then came the moment everyone had been waiting for - the judging of the new Silk Queen.

Above: Boys will be boys, and these two are obviously having a whale of a time splashing around in the flood waters. They might be enjoying themselves, but the situation that brightened their day with a little excitement was proving to be a real headache to their parents and neighbours gathered at the further end of the street. Streets awash with water was an unfortunate but familiar sight in and around the area known as The Dams. Elizabeth Street, possibly the subject of this photograph, was only one of the streets that was prone to flooding.

The big culprit was probably the occasional spell of prolonged rain or melting snow that caused a tributary of the River Bollin to overflow, and wet weather was no doubt dreaded by the luckless Maxonians whose homes were situated in The Dams. Raised barriers across the doorways, some of which can be seen in the photograph, were a common sight. Then of course when the flood water eventually subsided the mopping up operations began; the worst-affected homes must have been a sea of smelly mud that was messy to deal with and difficult to get rid of, not to mention being a drain on the purse of the insurance companies involved.

Below: Yes, it's 'Our Gracie' - but her New Year visit to Macclesfield in January 1948 was a private one; she had travelled up to see friends who lived in Prestbury. Gracie Fields nevertheless posed willingly for the camera, and the result was this delightfully informal snapshot taken outside her friends' home. Her husband Boris was, of course, with her - he is the man in the striped suit.

Born in 1898 as Grace Stansfield, the well-known and well-loved Rochdale-born actress and singer had played in music halls from childhood, and her role as Sally Perkins in 'Mr Tower of London' made her famous. Her voice charmed thousands, and 'My Blue Heaven', 'Sally' and 'The Biggest Aspidistra in the World' were the popular songs of the day. Her great appeal lay in her naturalness and down-to-earth manner as well as in her regional accent which she never lost. Eventually Gracie fled to the warmer climes of Italy and set up home in the hills of the beautiful island of Capri where she and her husband opened a restaurant. She gave nine command performances between 1928 and 1964, and became Dame Gracie Fields in 1979, the year of her death.

Above: A memorable scene in Waters Green was captured for posterity when at the end of World War II the Macclesfield Home Guard assembled for their final parade - and a fine-looking band of well-drilled men they were. When they first signed up, most of them had never before wielded so much as a broom handle in anger, but they were all prepared to do their bit for Britain.

At the start of the war Sir Anthony Eden, Secretary of State for War, appealed in a radio broadcast for men between 17 and 65 to make up a new force, the Local Defence Volunteers, to guard vulnerable points from possible Nazi attack. Within an hour the first men were putting their names down. At first the new force had to improvise; there were no weapons to spare and men had to rely on sticks and shotguns handed in by local people, and weapons and uniforms did not become available for several months. The Local Defence Volunteers was later renamed the Home Guard. Television programmes such as 'Dad's Army' have unfortunately associated the Home Guard with comedy, but even if amateur they were very well organised and performed much important work, posting sentries to watch for possible aircraft or parachute landings, manning anti-aircraft rocket guns, setting up communications and organising balloon barrages.

Right: The flags fly high in Bollington, and neighbours stand in their doorways to watch as this parade passes by. The exact occasion and date of the photograph is unknown, but it was almost certainly taken after the end of World War II, in the late 1940s. The young women marching proudly in the foreground are thought to be part of the local Queen Alexandra Nursing Corps, and we can speculate that the event was the official opening of the Remembrance Gardens - though from this distance in time we can not now be certain.

Originally part of Prestbury Parish, Bollington became a parish in its own right when St John's church was consecrated in 1834. By 1851, the year of the Great Exhibition, its population had risen to around 5,000. Bollington established itself as a textile town, with five large mills and a number of smaller ones, where both cotton and silk were produced. Demand for textiles gradually fell off after the second world war, however, and in spite of diversifying into the production of the modern synthetic fibres, all the town's mills closed during the 1970s. A few were given over to new uses while others gradually decayed and fell victim to demolition.

It was 2nd October 1929, and the town had turned out to give a right royal welcome to Henry, Duke of Gloucester, when he visited Macclesfield for the official opening of the Trentabank Reservoir at Langley. Waiting at Macclesfield Town Hall to welcome the Prince to the town was the Mayor, Councillor Fred Wood, and Brigadier General Sir William Bromley Davenport KCB. At the reservoir the Duke unlocked the gates with a golden key and ceremonially turned on the valves, declaring the Trentabank Reservoir open. The new reservoir, built by the Macclesfield Corporation Water Works (later North West Water), was a much-needed facility in the area. The chairman of the Waterworks Committee was Alderman John Hyde JP.

Prince Henry, the fourth child of six born to King George V and Queen Mary, was born in 1900. His oldest brother Edward, known to the family as 'David', became King Edward VIII, later abdicating to marry American divorcee Wallis Simpson and leaving the throne to our Queen's father, his brother Albert, who was next in line and became King George VI. Henry, Duke of Gloucester, died in 1974.

Above: A lot of party hats are in evidence among this group of residents in the Commercial Road area of Macclesfield, and a spirited 'knees-up' is possibly about to follow as the party celebrates VE day. The photograph shows a large number of older people - thoughtfully provided with seats in the foreground of the picture - who have just lived through yet another world war. They had all seen some tough times in their lives, and the tough times had not yet ended, as they were to find out. Rationing, for example, was to remain a part of British life until 1954. After the end of World War II there was no immediate let up in rationing, as many had hoped - in fact a year later in 1946 bread went on ration.

These particular residents, however, were on the threshold of many changes in the town. The terraces of houses where they had lived as a community for much of their lives were to fall victim to the demand for new housing in the town. Their homes were demolished and Victoria Park flats (themselves destined for demolition) were built in their place. The trees in the background of the photograph are believed to be in Victoria Park.

Above right: Pub trips are perennially popular, and this time the destination of the regulars at Ye Olde Swan With Two Necks was Ilkley Moor - a change from those regular trips to Blackpool, Morecambe or Rhyl. What did they do there, we have to wonder; the footwear of these trippers betrays the fact that they were not planning to spend the day tramping the hills! But the moors are rich in dramatic scenery and bracing fresh air, and Ilkley itself is to this day a pleasant little town; no doubt some time was spent in browsing in the shops, taking afternoon tea in one of the town's many tearooms - and no doubt calling in for a little evening refreshment at some popular hostelry on the way home. The date of the trip is not known, but judging by the square shoulders of the ladies coats and their just-below-the-knee length, this photograph would have been taken some time in the late 1940s.

The Swan, as the pub was called at the turn of the century, was bought by Adshead's Brewery in 1900. More recently Ye Olde Swan was given a thorough facelift and in 1970 was renamed the Chester Gate.

Above: If you are old enough to have listened to the radio during the 1940s, you will not have forgotten 'Have a Go' - and the tuneful little ditty that played in its presenter, Halifax born Wilfred Pickles: 'Have a go, Joe, come on and have a go....' Fifty years or so ago, the well-known and loved presenter 's programme topped the popularity lists with listeners all over the country, and Violet Carson, the show's pianist, had become a household name long before her role as *Coronation Street*'s Ena Sharples! Not only could the ordinary person in the street become a contestant on the show, he (or she) also stood the chance of returning home with a few extra pounds in his pocket, as 'Give him the money, Barney' was Pickles' well-known catchphrase.

When Wilfred Pickles brought his show to Macclesfield on November 17th 1949 an enthusiastic audience crammed into the Town Hall to take part in the programme. With Pickles in this nostalgic photograph is Mrs Dinah Shrigley, aged 84, while to his left is contestant twelve and a half year old Marie Buxton. In the days of the BBC's strictly plummy voices, Wilfred Pickles' down-to-earth Yorkshire accent was refreshingly ordinary. However did he get the job?

> **'GIVE HIM THE MONEY, BARNEY' WAS WILFRED PICKLES' WELL-KNOWN CATCHPHRASE**

You can almost hear the complaints of the children, can't you? 'Daddy - I can't see!' In the 1930s as now, children wanted to see everything that was going on, and Dads the world over have always been ready to provide a shoulder to give their child a grandstand view of an exciting event. There was plenty of excitement on the day of the Macclesfield carnival parade, as this delightful photograph reveals, and vast crowds have lined the streets and filled the open space of Park Green to watch the procession go by.

The parade of marchers, bands and colourful floats has just made its way along Sunderland Street and into Park Green, from where it will process up Park Street and into Park Lane to South Park, where the new Silk Queen will be chosen.

All the proceeds from the event went to Macclesfield Infirmary, and those nurses who could be spared from their duties for a day acted as fund-raisers and sportingly passed among the crowds rattling their collecting boxes.

Below: The election of the Silk Queen, her princesses, pages and retinue, each one gorgeously dressed in silk, was the high point of the Macclesfield Carnival. The name of this Silk Queen has disappeared in the mists of time, but her crowning must have been a very proud moment in her life. The Mayor of Macclesfield is very grand in his mayoral chain, glossy top hat and spats. For the benefit of our younger readers who may not have come across this particular item of gentlemen's clothing before, spats were a type of gaiter that covered the wearer's ankle and the top of the shoe.

Every mill would enter its own Silk Princess in the Carnival, their elaborately decorated floats forming part of the procession. The entire town was involved in the Carnival in one way or another, making costumes, decorating the floats, constructing the props or taking part in the procession. The event was a red-letter day in Macclesfield's calendar, and those people who played no active part in the occasion would turn out to watch, wave and cheer as the parade made its way past them towards South Park.

Right: With flowers in their hair and smiles of genuine enjoyment on their faces these mill workers (aided and abetted by a glass or three from the bottles on the table!) were obviously having a whale of a time. The event being celebrated is not clear; the party could have been held to mark the Queen's coronation in 1953, though on reflection it was more likely to have been Christmas time.

The warm jumpers and cardigans and the type of decorations are more in keeping with Christmas - and the photograph is rather lacking in red, white and blue stripes and patriotic flags. But whatever the occasion, the refreshments generously provided by the management clearly made this a very memorable party. How many of these lady workers had sore heads the following morning? A bottle of Gilbey's Sherry occupies a prominent place in the centre of the table, while Mackeson's milk stout was also popular among the ladies. And is that a half-empty whisky bottle in the background?

Below: The riot of seasonal flowers decorating the tables cannot hide the gleaming well-deserved trophies proudly displayed at the front of the room. The trophies, together with the dates 1901 and 1951 displayed at the front of the dining room are evidence that this was a special occasion. This was, in fact, the Macclesfield and District Football Association's 50th birthday celebration, and the Jubilee Dinner was given in the Masonic Hall. The President of the FA, James Wilson, was in the chair for the occasion, and guests at the dinner included officials and players from all the local clubs. Among the guests is Macclesfield Times reporter Eric Dunkley (third from centre on the right, with a small moustache). He would presumably have been there to report the event - a pleasant task, no doubt, when the assignment included a good dinner!

The town subsequently lost the Macclesfield Times, but many readers will remember the popular paper.

THE MACCLESFIELD & DISTRICT FOOTBALL ASSOCIATION'S 50TH BIRTHDAY DINNER WAS HELD AT THE MASONIC HALL

Above: It seems very strange to look back at a Chestergate with traffic, and Chestergate in the photograph was resplendent with flags and bunting, garlands and banners in honour of the Queen's coronation in 1953.

There were few television aerials on the roofs of buildings back then, and though Britain had a television service as early as 1936, few people could afford to buy one of the very expensive TV sets - and the range of programmes was very limited anyway. Many early sets had very small screens, and it was possible to buy a specially-made magnifying glass which fitted over the front of the screen and made viewing more comfortable. By the 1950s sets were beginning to get cheaper, and the Queen's coronation presented many families with the ideal reason to buy or rent a TV set. Those who did not simply crowded into the parlours of more fortunate neighbours to watch the event!

The news on the morning of the coronation carried other news that the world had been waiting for - New Zealander Edmund Hillary, with John Hunt and Sherpa Tensing, had reached the summit of Everest. The 'Daily Express' headline said it all: 'All this and Everest Too'.

Maxonians turned out en masse to watch the coronation march held in June 1953, lining the route of the parade to cheer the marchers on their way, sitting their flag-waving young children on their shoulders to get a better view of the exciting event that had been in preparation for some weeks past. It is interesting to take note of the prevailing fashions of the day worn by the crowd in Chestergate and the marchers as they pass the offices of the Macclesfield Advertiser and Williams and Deacon's Bank. The Ladies' Choir, though wearing light summery clothes were nevertheless very proper with their little hats, handbags and, of course, the obligatory gloves without which no young woman felt properly dressed even as recently as the 1950s. The vast majority of the men are wearing hats.

Perhaps a few people among the crowd would have been able to watch the crowning of the Queen in Westminster Abbey on television; it was the first time the coronation of a British monarch had ever been filmed, and the whole event was carefully timed to within thirty seconds.

Below: Fifty thousand people turned out to greet Princess Elizabeth and Prince Philip, who had married just two years earlier, when they visited Macclesfield on 27th June 1949. Hibel Road Station was a riot of colourful blooms when the royal train steamed in at 10am, and Councillor F Fowler, the Mayor of Macclesfield, was waiting to formally receive the visitors. Outside, the crowds let themselves go as the couple appeared, and along the route to Market Place they cheered themselves hoarse. It was a beautiful day, and the town let itself go in a way it hadn't done since the end of World War II. Across the town flags and bunting fluttered gaily in the breeze, and banners proclaimed a whole-hearted welcome to the royal couple.

The Princess and Duke of Edinburgh had asked that their visit should include a tour of one of Macclesfield's silk mills, and Brocklehurst Whiston Amalgamated Ltd's Hurdsfield Mills was chosen for

the privilege. Princess Elizabeth was presented with two silk dress lengths - and was also given a box of silk handkerchiefs to take home for Prince Charles, born seven months previously.

On her father's death three years after her visit to Macclesfield, Princess Elizabeth became queen.

Bottom: Along with the rest of the town, Macclesfield Equitable and Provident Co-operative Society building took the opportunity of the Silver Jubilee of King George V and Queen Mary to state their patriotism, and flags flew from their every available flagstaff. The occasion was a country-wide party, and every town and village made their own plans to deck windows and doorways with red, white and blue garlands, hang bunting across every street and run up the Union Jack from every flagpole.

George, Duke of York, came to the throne in 1910. The model of the ideal Englishman, King George made himself immensely popular with his subjects without really trying. He was tolerant of people whose opinions differed from his own - but not afraid to speak his mind when the occasion called for straight talking. Dignified, fair, conscientious and modest, he once remarked on the warmth with which people greeted him during his Silver Jubilee celebrations, 'I am beginning to think they like me for myself.' George V was the first monarch to broadcast the Christmas Day message which over the years became the established tradition that we still enjoy today. King George died in 1936; his widow, Queen Mary, lived on until 1953.

Above: It was 1953, coronation year, and all over Britain each town and city, every village institute and church, held their own event, which could range from a simple street party to a big parade. Maxonians, of course, were not backward in joining in the fun and refused to allow the steady drizzle that fell steadily on the day of the coronation to dampen their enthusiasm. Some street parties went ahead while alternative premises such as schools and church halls were hastily found for others. There was barely a window without its union jack and coloured bunting in Waterloo Street, where these happy residents were caught on camera. The names of many are known: from left to right are Mrs Hawkins with her grandson Robert Whittaker, the local postman whose name unfortunately is unknown, Myrtle Butterworth with her daughter Pam, Mrs and Mrs Selman, Mrs Sharpley alongside another neighbour, Mrs Fox and her son, Mr Sharpley, and Mrs Smith, who kept the corner shop, with another child. A great time, no doubt, was had by all.

Waterloo Street was later demolished along with surrounding streets to make way for the Victoria Park corporation flats.

Below: The Macclesfield Carnival, once a regular event penned into every Maxonian's diary, had been interrupted by the second world war. It was 20 years or so before Richard Porter and a group of other local residents campaigned to have the event revived. Their campaigning finally paid off, and the Macclesfield Carnival finally made a comeback in the 1960s. A few cameras can be seen among the watching crowd who assembled in front of the Town Hall to watch the procession get underway. Sitting in the centre of the photograph is Alderman Mrs Lily Davenport JP, the Mayor of Macclesfield, who had been given the dubious pleasure of judging the merits of the various floats. This was Mrs Davenport's second term as Mayor, having been elected during the Charter Year, 1961. The lady sitting on her left is Mrs Davenport's sister, who was Mayoress of Macclesfield.

Charter Year had been a key occasion in Macclesfield; 700 years earlier Prince Edward Earl of Chester, later King Edward I, had granted the Charter to the Burgesses of Macclesfield, making the town a free borough with a merchant guild and many other privileges. Edward signed the Charter on 29th May 1261.

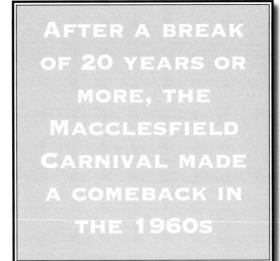

AFTER A BREAK OF 20 YEARS OR MORE, THE MACCLESFIELD CARNIVAL MADE A COMEBACK IN THE 1960S

Left: 'Long live Queen Elizabeth II' proclaims the huge sign at the Christ Church Coronation Pageant that was held back in June, 1953. Macclesfield was not alone, of course, in rejoicing in the 'New Elizabethan' age - the Queen's coronation was an opportunity for Britons around the country to state their patriotism - and an excuse for a country-wide party. Every town and village made their own plans to deck windows and doorways with red, white and blue garlands, hang bunting across every street, run up the Union Jack from every flagpole and plan street parties for all the local kids. Dances were held, shows were staged, fireworks displays were put on and new songs were composed to celebrate the occasion - perhaps readers will remember 'Let's all be new Elizabethans'? Though most of the children here will now be in their mid-fifties, perhaps some readers will recognise themselves as the Elizabethans in this photograph taken so long ago, and will maybe find memories of this happy occasion flooding back.

Above: Readers in their middle years should look closely at this delightful school photograph taken in the early 1950s - they may be surprised to spot themselves as they were, aged around six! The school was Trinity Square Primary, and there are more than a few mischievous smiles on the faces of these little cuties.

The class looks a good deal more relaxed than similar group photographs taken around the turn of the century. That could be due in part to the necessity of standing absolutely still for those earlier cameras; children inclined to fidget were told to stand still and 'watch the birdie'. No birdie was forthcoming, of course, to the disappointment of many a child, but the ploy usually did the trick in making them look at the camera! The whole atmosphere surrounding this more recent class is quite different, however. Was it due to a relaxation of the once-rigid school discipline, and the fear of the dreaded cane? Or could it be that school had become a far more interesting place to be? Sadly, we will never know the answer. Trinity Square School was eventually demolished to make way for the Victoria Park flats complex.

We can only guess at the colours of the flowers that went into this beautiful arrangement that adorned Hibel Road Station on 27th June 1949, but the display must have been a memorable sight. Princess Elizabeth and Prince Philip were expected in Macclesfield that day, and the royal couple must surely have been impressed by the riot of colour as their train steamed into the station at ten in the morning. The identity of the three young ladies in the picture remains a mystery, however. Who were they, and why were they pictured with the flower arrangements? At a guess we might deduce that they were the creators of this lovely display, and if so, we must pay tribute to their artistic talent.

On the platform waiting to greet the royal visitors was the Mayor of Macclesfield, Councillor F Fowler, and as they left the station the Duke of Edinburgh inspected a unit of the Seventh Cheshire Regiment. It was a proud day for local schoolgirl Shirley Hankinson, who was chosen to present a bouquet to the Princess on behalf of all Macclesfield's schoolchildren, who turned out in full force to view the royal procession.

Sporting life

> **IN THE CHESHIRE LEAGUE DAYS IT WAS NORMAL TO SEE BETWEEN FIVE AND SIX THOUSAND FANS AT A MATCH**

A sight to bring back many fond memories to supporters who turned out in their thousands to watch the Silkmen from this stand; in those Cheshire League days it was normal to see crowds of between 5,000 to 6,000 at a match. The old stand was demolished in the 1960s and was replaced by an ultra-modern cantilever stand. This wonderful old photograph was taken at a Macclesfield v Rhyl game during the 1940s, and the young lads who sat around the edge of the pitch to get a good view on the day this scene was caught on camera will now be in their late 50s. Will any reader recognise himself as one of these enthusiastic youngsters, one wonders? The game was much more laid-back in those days; can you imagine children being allowed to sit on the pitch today?

In the background towards the right, all wearing trilby hats, are the four Murray brothers, who were well-known figures in the town. Philip Murray was a reporter on the Macclesfield Times; an ardent supporter of Macclesfield FC, his other passion was for fly fishing, for which sport he won many trophies.

Above: The lads of local team Northern Athletic back in the 1953 - 1954 season assemble for a formal team photograph with team manager W Crowder standing on the right. The names of the team will be of interest locally: from left to right standing, G Hewitt, G Crowder, P Jones, F Roberts, B Wilson, G Batten, F Corners, F Stonely and manager W Crowder in the raincoat. In front are K Simpson, J Wood, F Lawson, P Barnett and J Cooper. Northern Athletic were very successful in their day, but were later disbanded.

Note the leather Casey ball the team played with. The leather ball had an inner inflated bladder and in contrast to the light plastic ball used today were very heavy. Players who headed the ball in those days were deserving of real admiration! Note, too, the strip, with shirts that fastened with a cord at the neck.

Above right: An interesting story lies behind this photograph, which commemorates a piece of daftness which nevertheless demanded superb fitness and stamina. Here Russell Wright is congratulated by the Mayor of Buxton after he had completed a memorable walk from Macclesfield to Buxton. Nothing amazing about that, some may say - until they discover that the walk was accomplished backwards! Think of the tremendous effort involved in using muscles

seldom used to walk long distances...most of us would never think of attempting it.

It all started back in the 1800s when Maxonian John Alcock took it into his head to bet his cronies in the Oxford Road Tavern that he could walk backwards from Macclesfield to Buxton. Not slow to recognise a golden opportunity to gain a bob or two, they took him up on it - but of course John won his bet. Several years later he repeated his walk, knocking 15 minutes off his previous time. It was around 100 years later that Russell Wright, a member of the Macclesfield Harriers, decided to revive the walk. In 1950 he successfully completed the backwards feat and afterwards was photographed with the Mayor. Ten years or so later he repeated his success. Subsequently the Macclesfield Lions organised regular backwards charity walks.

The whole town went wild with joy and turned out in their hundreds to give the lads a well-deserved welcome home in January 1968, when Macclesfield FC played First Division team Fulham in the third round of the FA Cup. Market Place was wall-to-wall with cheering, waving supporters that day - and the smiles on the faces in the crowd say it all. The banner in the background has nothing to do with politics, of course - Macc's popular local hero, defender John Collins, was dubbed 'Minister of Defence' for the occasion. The game was a memorable one; captained by Macclesfield solicitor Keith Goalen (an appropriate name!), the small team were winning at half-time. The bubble burst in the second half, however - and the rest is history. They were robbed - and on their return Maxonians turned out in force to tell them so.

Readers may have spotted Richard Porter (left of centre in the foreground, wearing glasses) among the crowd. A well-known FC supporter, he worked with Macclesfield Hospital for many years.

From the same standpoint, the view taken in Market Place has changed over the years. T Seymour Mead's Grocery store has disappeared, and Boots the Chemist is now, of course, in the Grosvenor Shopping Centre.

Wartime

Steadily-falling rain could not dampen the enthusiasm of the crowd who turned out to watch the Cheshire Regiment's civic march-past, though the Town Clerk Walter Isaac was well-protected by a large black umbrella. Though we are not sure of the actual date of this photograph, the march-past took place shortly after the end of the second world war in 1945, when people gathered to welcome home the returning troops.

During the war parades had become an accepted part of life; children loved the excitement of the rousing bands and the marching soldiers, and they undoubtedly made the average person in the street feel in touch with the military and the progress of the war.

When war was declared in 1939 Macclesfield along with the rest of the country had rolled up its sleeves and prepared for the inevitable. Thousands of evacuees were absorbed into the town. Air raid shelters were hurriedly built in open spaces. Place names and other identifying marks were obscured to confuse the enemy about exactly where they were, and notices about wearing gas masks and careless talk went up everywhere. Now, they were simply glad that it was all over.

Both pictures: This display in the windows of the Co-op in Park Green during World War II emphasised the need for women workers to take jobs in the factories to replace those men who had been called into military service. The flying suit at the rear of one of the windows was probably made from rubberised silk, as was the dinghy in the other window. Parachutes, flags, and many other products were desperately needed for the offensive, and the sign 'You are wanted now to make these things' rammed the message home to passing ladies.

Clothing was also needed, and though many of their workers were called up Belmonts of Macclesfield (who prior to the war had been furriers) managed to keep going and found themselves turning out sheepskin coats for the Russian allies as well as for our own troops, scarves, flying helmets and battle dress. Other companies changed direction and became involved in war work; Backhouse and Coppock Ltd produced food packaging, wrappers, cartons - and 'window'. If you have read books like 'The Dam Busters' the term 'window' will be a familiar one. Nothing to do with panes of glass of course, but strips of aluminium foil which were dropped from allied planes during World War II to avoid detection by enemy radar. Backhouse and

Coppock produced more than thirty tons of window during the war.

Women were called upon to fill places in all industries during the second world war, and discovered talents and abilities they never knew they had.

Traditionally, British men have been regarded as the bread winners, going out to work every day to keep their wives and families. Their women folk saw to the children, shopped for food every day, made the meals, cleaned the house, and washed and ironed the family's clothes. The second world war changed the way of life for hundreds of men and women, turning generations of tradition upside down.

THE END OF THE WAR SAW THE COMING TOGETHER OF WHOLE COMMUNITIES IN A WAY RARELY SEEN

Above: It was 1945, and every Maxonian was tired of bombs, gas masks, the blackout and all the other privations of wartime Britain, and when peace was declared after six long years of war bunting was strung from house to house across every street, and patriotic flags flapped gaily in the breeze. Along with the rest of Britain, the people of Macclesfield found the energy to let their hair down and organise victory parades, street parties, fireworks displays and bonfires. The end of the war saw the coming together of whole communities in a way rarely seen, and this picture of happy children, their parents and neighbours enjoying sandwiches, jellies and cakes on 8th May - a warm sunny day - was repeated at scores of street parties organised around Macclesfield.

Both pictures: The war was over at long last, and out came the flags and the bunting, the coloured crepe paper and the scissors. The making of so many wonderful party hats must have resembled a scene from 'Blue Peter' (only without the sticky-backed plastic!). Communities went wild with joy when the news that everybody was waiting for was announced. It was good to be alive, and along with the rest of Britain the people from these Macclesfield streets, from the grandparents to the tiniest child found the energy to let their hair down and have a knees-up to celebrate victory in the time-honoured way - a street party. The strain of war is visible on several of the faces in these revealing photographs; perhaps they were among those whose family members or friends had been killed or injured, of which Macclesfield had its share. The town's war memorial was officially opened in 1920 to respect those who died in World War I; three years after the end of the second world war a wreath was ceremonially laid to honour those who gave their lives in this more recent conflict.

Above: This little party was probably one of the many held to celebrate victory at the end of the second world war. These smiling ladies, some straight from the kitchen and still wearing aprons or overalls, had clearly prepared a rather more sedate little tea party than many (notice the absence of children and the size of the table). Sandwiches, jam tarts and trifle are on the menu, perhaps made with ingredients that had been carefully hoarded for just such an event. Back in 1945 everyone was looking forward to an end to rationing and a more prosperous future.

It was Britain's new Prime Minister, Clement Attlee, who brought the nation down from its euphoria with a resounding bump. He gave the country a serious warning that although Britain was once more at peace, there was no likelihood of prosperity for the country in the immediate future. Across the world countries were decimated by war, and there were worldwide food shortages. It would be several more years before people could stop using tinned dried eggs or shop for clothes without counting how many coupons they had.

Right: 'God save the King'! proclaims the patriotic banner floating in the breeze in the background; in fact the people of Britain had developed a genuine fondness for the King and his beautiful Queen, who during the war had opted to stay in London with their people rather than remove to a place of safety. The royal couple even waived their privileges and insisted on wartime rationing along with the rest of the nation.

But now the war was over, and it was party time for Britain in general and Macclesfield in particular. The Town Hall was illuminated for the occasion, and hundreds of revellers in Market Place danced on far into the night, undeterred by the rain. Rarely had the words of 'Auld Lang Syne' echoed so sincerely around the streets of Macclesfield.

This happy photograph captures the euphoric mood of the residents of Dickens Street and Fence Street, who held their VE Day party in the playground of Daybrook Street school. When peace was declared after six long years of war this wonderful scene of joy was repeated in every street across the length and breadth of Great Britain.

An establishment famous for furniture

For nearly 150 years, the name of Arighi Bianchi has been synonymous with high quality furniture, and inextricably associated with the town of Macclesfield. Its history is a long and fascinating one and begins with two hard working Italians leaving turbulent times of civil war in Tuscany to find a new life in England.

Antonio Arighi was the first to arrive in 1854, aged eighteen, having made the long journey from his home in Casnate, a small village near Camerlata in the Italian province of Como. It must have been a long, hard and arduous journey through the St Gothard pass into Switzerland. Not too much is known about the details but it is understood that most of the journey was negotiated on foot.

If details of this dramatic trek are now lost in the mists of time, we can at least feel certain why Macclesfield was chosen as the eventual destination. Casnate, the place of Antonio's birth, was a village devoted to silk working and the Cheshire town was of course known throughout Europe for its excellence in the same industry.

Soon after his arrival, Antonio took premises on Waters Green and started in business. He began by making clocks and barometers, which he hawked around the neighbouring countryside in search of customers. Rising at five in the morning he would trudge many miles each day sometimes as far as Biddulph and the Potteries in an effort to sell his wares. Despite his poor grasp of English, it seems he was seldom unlucky. Legend had it that his persuasive skills were second to none, and somewhat ingenious. Hardheaded local farmers were reluctant to yield a farthing of their hard-earned cash and would generally express no interest in Antonio's craftsmanship. The young man would accept these knock-backs graciously and sigh that he must therefore bear everything back home to Macclesfield. Then an idea would apparently strike him: he wondered, he would say, if the farmer might perhaps look after one of the barometers until he was next in the area? It would at least mean one less thing to carry. The farmer would naturally agree. Weeks later, Antonio would return. By this time, the farmer

Below: The elegant days of furniture delivery by horse drawn vehicle, with Francis Arighi second left (hands on hips).

It was during this period that cabinet making almost certainly became the main area of interest, and clearly succeeded, for within a few short years the business transferred to more commodious premises on Waters Green by Buxton Bridge where it could take advantage of workrooms, warehouses, showroom, stable, outbuildings and a cabinet maker's shop.

had become so dependent on the device that he couldn't bear to part with it, and would offer to pay for it on the spot!

Picture framing was soon added to the business and Antonio Arighi's reputation grew. By 1861 he had premises at Oldham's place (behind Cookson's garage, at the side of the bus station today), and had been joined by three assistants, two from Italy and John Broadhurst, a native of Macclesfield.

By 1868 Antonio Bianchi, in his early twenties and a cabinetmaker by trade, joined the firm. He also came from Casnate, having recently married Teresa, Antonio Arighi's niece.

Above: Past members of the family: Top (left to right) John Bianchi, Antonio Bianchi, Francis Arighi and bottom (left to right) Enrico Bianchi, Sydney Bianchi, Alphonso Bianchi. *Below:* A delivery cart outside the Mill Road premises showing Antonio Bianchi in the driving seat!

Disaster struck in 1872 when great floods in Macclesfield, the worst for one hundred years, caused the River Bollin to break its banks inflicting substantial damage on timber, veneering and other valuable materials. It was probably of some relief, therefore, that the business soon afterwards accepted an offer from the Railway Company who were eager to widen the approach to their new station as part of the construction of the Macclesfield, Bollington and Marple railway.

New and drier premises were quickly found at 42 Mill Road, Sutton, and before long Antonio Arighi and Antonio Bianchi became official partners, at the head of the thriving enterprise. From daybooks of the time, we learn that most customers lived locally but orders were already coming in from as far afield as the Potteries, Buxton and Manchester. One contemporary order even came from Llandudno - listing two men's railway fares, together with instructions to remove furniture and to lay linoleum, providing for four days work at 2/6d (12 1/2p) per day. By 1877 the most popular goods on sale at the shop were Mahogany Pembroke tables and painted iron bedsteads with mattresses of straw, feather and hair. Mahogany furniture features promi-nently, alongside Brussels carpets, French bedsteads, dressers and tables crafted in walnut and oak. Upholstery and soft furnishings were increasingly in evidence; a new home could be entirely fitted out, then as now, in a single visit to Arighi Bianchi.

The success of their life in England did not, however, mean that the Italian compatriots lost touch with their roots. Indeed, there is evidence that Antonio Arighi returned to Italy in 1879. Whether this was the start of a prolonged stay or simply the first in a series of visits is not clear. Suffice it to say that consignments of furniture (and even an order for toy prams) were delivered to him in Casnate at various times over the next few years, although by the end of the century he was firmly ensconced back in Macclesfield, living at 6 Beech Lane with his wife Guilia and daughters Esther, Alice and Edvige.

Expansion continued apace, and within a decade new premises were in demand. In 1883, Arighi Bianchi opened for business at its new premises in the Commercial Road Silk Mill. The silk

Below: As time progressed the motor vehicle gradually superseded horse drawn transport, and Arighi Bianchi were the first to own and operate this commercial delivery vehicle - offering free delivery within a 30 mile radius and seen here driven by Edward Connolly who was later killed in action at the Somme, April 1915.

industry, as a source of employment for the area, had changed dramatically in the course of the 19th century. Commercial Road had once been at its heart, but a decline in handloom weaving, particularly after the introduction of power looms and notably the revolutionary Jacquard loom of 1820, followed by stiff competition from France, saw only 13% of businesses in the road still occupied in silk by the 1870s (compared with 58% in the 1820s). Retail trading had become the focus of activity and the Silk Mill's new role as the home of Arighi Bianchi was in many respects a change that fitted the times.

But many may have considered the Mill a far-from-ideal acquisition. In poor condition, the floors were perilously uneven and only one storey, at ground level, was suitable for public use. Still, the firm was quick to make the most of its potential, contracting George Roylance, a local builder with property of his own in the vicinity, to erect a new shop front. The improvement vastly improved matters. Resplendent with long rows of windows on three floors, there was now ample opportunity for generous displays of the company's wares and the upper two storeys of the mill were swiftly pressed into service as storage areas. The Company's move to its new home was widely advertised in the local press and opened its doors for the first time in December 1883.

Ten years later George Roylance was called upon again but this time to construct a brand new four-storey building next to the existing mill. It survives to this day as an impressive testament, both to the artistic vision and to the commercial success of Arighi and Bianchi in Victorian England. With a facade inspired by Joseph Paxton's famous Crystal Palace for the 1851 Great Exhibition, it made an immediate impact on both the architectural appeal of the town and the refined sensibilities of its inhabitants when it

opened in 1892. A journalist from the Macclesfield Courier and Herald caught the mood:

'The front of the building is an artistic combination of large plate glass windows in light iron ornamental frames, with a handsome doorway in polished mahogany laid with ornate tiles, the name of the firm being worked in the centre. The whole building is so arranged as to be lighted by a splendid centre light in the roof, the light from which is reflected down the staircase which forms a sort of gallery, thus casting a beautifully subdued light into the lower rooms so that the furniture is seen to greater advantage.'

The ground floor was devoted to drawing, and dining-room furniture, much of it solid and inlaid fancy woods, and a variety of knick knacks, including mirrors, hat stands, plaques etc, together with library and office furniture. On the first floor, reached by way of a fantastic Oregon pine staircase decorated with ornamental items, were to be found bedroom furniture and draperies. The second floor offered cheaper bedroom suites for the servants' rooms of gentlemen's houses and for artisans, whilst the third housed unfinished furniture waiting to be seasoned. An extensive drapery department, stocked with everything from lace curtains to tapestries, completed the new building's extensive wares.

The company was now fully fledged, a large concern with an enviable reputation growing across the country and offering goods (in a quaint phrase of the time) 'to suit all classes'.

Next to arrive on the scene was another member of the family, Francis Arighi, who was the nephew of Antonio Arighi and brother of Teresa. After a spell in Chicago (selling oysters and fruit

Above: An estimate for replacement flooring at the Commercial Road Silk Mill in 1889.

from his barrow!), he returned to Italy but then travelled to Macclesfield and soon became a partner and the Company name changed to Arighi, Bianchi & Co. Frank, as he was affectionately known, took an active part in the business life of the community. In 1902 he was on the executive committee of the Macclesfield and District Tradesman's Association, now the Chamber of Trade and between 1912 and 1933

Frank was chairman of the Company. He died in 1933, aged 72, never having married.

In 1900, at the dawn of a new century, the firm was established as a Limited Company, and deeds relating to this development reveal a significant shift in the founders' allegiance. From this time onwards, they each came to be known not as Antonio, but as Anthony. The future, it seemed,

rested forever in their adopted home of Cheshire. It wasn't long before the business could afford yet more expansion when Arighi Bianchi opened a second store in Spring Gardens, Buxton, and an additional outlet had appeared in Wilmslow by 1905.

In the early 1900s Arighi Bianchi's transport depended on horses, which became the pride and joy of Anthony Bianchi. He would arrive at the company stables every morning before breakfast to supervise their grooming and wait in the evening until the last horse had returned. (The stables survive, and today they are an important feature of the building, nestled behind the bed linen and nursery department).

Complete home removals were also offered at this time, and Arighi Bianchi horse-drawn vans were a familiar sight on the roads for a number of years. Later on, Arighi Bianchi was to own and operate the very first motorised commercial vehicle in Macclesfield. The firm was able to provide free delivery up to a radius of thirty miles, and attracted nationwide, indeed worldwide, custom by promising to attend to orders arriving by post on the very day when they were received.

News of this remarkable company soon reached the ears of Royalty. Orders and receipts exist for goods sent to Marlborough House and Sandringham when Edward VII was Prince of Wales. Among these orders was one from Princess Alexandra, later the Queen, for a pair of carved oak candlesticks priced at £2.9s. Unfortunately when Queen Mary ordered two further pairs some years later the price had risen to £4.9s per pair!

As the years passed, Anthony Bianchi took to looking down from his home on Brunswick Hill to his Commercial Road premises, keeping a vigilant eye on all that went on. Anthony and Teresa had seven children, five sons and two daughters. Enrico born 1880 who married Marjorie but had no children; Clara born 1886 married John Clayton and had one daughter, Margaret; Sidney who was born in 1883 was unmarried and died in London aged 24 of tuberculosis.

Left: A fair in the centre of town at the turn of the century, with an Arighi Bianchi advertising hoarding taking a very prominent position.

He was a designer for Gillows, the famous furniture manufacturers; Alfonso, born 1893, unmarried and died aged 32 of tuberculosis following active service with the Royal Engineers; Josephine born 1892, unmarried; Leo died aged 2 years old; John Bianchi born 1896 and died in 1992 married Irene Mary Whitehead who produced two sons, John Anthony and Robert Paul. This is the only line which is still in existence today.

Anthony Bianchi (the co-founder) died in 1911 at the age of 65; Francis then became Chairman of the company in 1912.

The First World War was a particularly harsh time, seeing the loss of many loyal employees. At this time John was pursuing a career in engineering and volunteered for the Navy and Alfonso joined the Royal Engineers leaving Enrico to carry on the business.

The period after the First World War saw the firm diversifying under the enthusiasm of Enrico Bianchi who himself became Chairman in 1933. Arighi Bianchi had developed a fine reputation for their vast range of imported materials from all over continental Europe, including tapestries, damasks, cretonnes, lace and velvet, but Enrico went one better by designing and printing his own creations. So successful was this wholesale division that by the mid 1930s this side of the business had all but overwhelmed the furniture interests and in fact these were only to survive because Enrico's youngest brother, John Ernest, expressed a desire to keep them going.

Antiques were also a passion of Enrico, and he leased the Priest's House in Prestbury (now the National Westminster Bank), soon to become his showroom for antiques, which he supplied throughout the country.

The outbreak of World War II saw the end of the wholesale fabric division and one final consignment was sunk on a ship bound for South America.

Cabinet making itself was not to last. The last cabinetmaker was Walter Skellern, and when he died, he took with him skills that were never to be replaced.

After the War business was at an all time low, but Enrico and John energetically set about building the business once more. WK Lowe Knitwear Limited leased the old premises, and a small branch shop was opened in Chestergate to capture passing trade, as the Commercial Road site had very little at this time.

The firm's centenary in 1954 was widely celebrated, and in the following year John's sons Anthony and Paul joined the firm and began to play an active role in the business.

Enrico died in 1956 and that year Mr John, as he was respectfully known, succeeded as chairman, in a role he held until his death in 1992 aged 96.

Anthony and Paul had no illusions about the task which lay ahead. The once famous business needed an injection of capital, vision and vigour. The former was helped by the acquisition by WK Lowe, of the original Commercial Road Silk Mill. Refurbishments were carried out including a new rear entrance, and a lift was installed. Curtain and upholstery workrooms were moved to the top floor.

Gradually, as goods became more available and contacts renewed, and new sources investigated,

Above: A selection of past advertisements and invoices dating back to 1875.

Transport acquired their property.

Anthony and Paul instigated a petition to save the building and many hundreds of signatures were obtained. It was so heartening for them to hear the views of loyal customers and they were overwhelmed by their support. This action brought recognition as to the architectural importance of the building. It was profoundly disturbing for the firm to discover that the premises had no listing under statutory legislation that might afford it protection (nor indeed did any other building in Macclesfield at this time).

Hopes were fading fast despite valiant efforts made across the land by The Architectural Review, The Victorian Society and even Sir John Betjeman.

a steady period of growth began. This could not have happened without the wonderful support of loyal customers who returned once again, and the small team of dedicated staff, without whose help this growth could never have been attempted.

It was at this time that the shop in the centre of the town was refurbished and entirely devoted to linens and furnishing fabrics and was looked after by Mr John and Mrs Oldfield, the company secretary and longest serving employee (previous secretary to Enrico Bianchi). All the beautifully written Sale tickets were the work of Mr John who took great pride in the shop, until the early 1980s, when the department was transferred to Commercial Road.

In 1970 the long talked about North South Macclesfield relief road reared its head once again and Arighi Bianchi was served a compulsory purchase order, and was instructed to find new premises. Legal advice was sought, and the opinion was that nothing could be done to prevent the scheme from going ahead. Therefore Anthony and Paul decided to take matters into their own hands, and fought singlehandedly to preserve the property.

Neighbours WK Lowe were offered a new site in Pickford Street, and the Department of

There was at last a happy ending. While on the one hand, one Government Office was doing its best to demolish the building, the Home of Arighi Bianchi was saved by another Government Office who at the eleventh hour granted a Grade II Listing with Star.

During the battle to save the building, Nicholas Winterton MP played a huge part and his never ending determination and support during such a bleak time will always be remembered by the Company.

The Ministry of Transport at the time indicated the road would not be constructed for at least two years (this was in 1973). It took a further twenty years to become a reality! The original building, now owned by the Department of Transport, was resold to the Company and Arighi Bianchi was back exactly where it was one hundred years ago.

Another period of expansion followed this crisis - an essential storage space was taken up on Sunderland Street (the home of Scraggs Textile Engineering firm) and carpet workrooms were found in Bollington. The Company was back in flourishing form.

Anthony's son Richard arrived in the early 1980s, followed by his brothers John and William. Paul's son Robert and daughter Sarah also joined. With

the site now safe from developers, significant building work was undertaken. The Coffee Shop was opened in 1988 and rapidly garnered a host of prestigious awards. Storage space was acquired in 1989 in Old Park Lane (the ex Halles textile mill) and the firm's fleet of vehicles expanded to service the increased demand.

Development work has continued ever since, in response to a renewed enthusiasm amongst customers for the complete shopping experience. A Nursery department was inaugurated, and most recently, a new reception area introduced, together with an enlarged bedlinen and bedroom furniture department.

Nowadays, traditional values of service and quality are offered across a staggering array of products in over thirty separate showrooms. Leading brands of furniture, fabric and carpets from top manufacturers across Europe are available, supported by a complementary interior design service. Eighteen full time carpet fitters and twenty three full time seamstresses ensure that a customer's individual needs are expertly catered for, and a recent innovation has brought Arighi Bianchi's exclusive brand of furniture crafted by the very best manufacturers and unavailable elsewhere, to the heart of the store.

THE FUTURE

There can be few businesses left that are still being actually run by the immediate descendants of the original owner. Fewer still that are looking forward with relish to beginning their 3rd Century of trading. Arighi Bianchi is one of them

Top left: The beautifully lit interior of the store as we know it today. ***Below:*** *A night time view of Arighi Bianchi.*

and what makes it all the more remarkable is that despite the economic struggles and political strife it was founded by two Italian immigrants with a limited grasp of the English language.

A new generation of Bianchis are now truly established and all are immersed in the traditional trading ethics handed down from when Antonio was plying his trade to the local farmers. However, this is not to say that this is an inward looking company, as a financial director, Robert Densem, the first ever non Arighi or Bianchi director, was appointed to cope with the ever changing retail world. This has enabled Mr Anthony and Mr Paul to concentrate on trading issues.

The yearning desire to expand has never faltered and plans are in place to restore the whole site to its former glory, with of course ample provision for parking to complement Macclesfield's Council scheme for redevelopment of Victoria Park.

Who knows, by the time you have read this, work could well be underway!

As it stands today, Richard and Robert manage most of the sales and marketing while John and William oversee the administration and transport.

In time, the family look forward to welcoming Sarah back to full time employment once her children, Lucy and James reach school age.

Nick is currently developing his own career in the food industry.

All things being equal the Company is well equipped for the challenges of the future backed by a highly prized team, of now over one hundred and fifty all dedicated to providing a high standard of personal service and creating a relaxed and friendly environment.

This remarkable family business, unique in its way, has travelled a long road since the days when young men tramped the Cheshire lanes with clocks and barometers, armed only with a smattering of English, quick-witted intelligence, and a determination to succeed. But succeed they did and fashioned what has in time become an internationally famous firm, proud of its noble past and looking forward to a sound, well-furnished future.

Above: The Bianchi family 1999: Back row (left to right) Sarah, Paul, Anthony, John and front row (left to right) Nicholas, Robert, William and Richard. Below: Arighi Bianchi into the 21st Century. A computer illustration showing the proposed extension (left side).

Around the town centre

Above: This wonderful pigeon's eye view of Macclesfield captures a moment frozen in time. Arbourhay Street and the surrounding area holds many memories for many Maxonians who were once part of the tightly-knit communities who lived there. These streets were all swept away to make room for the Victoria Park development, Macclesfield's answer to the town's housing shortage. But pride in the new project was short-lived and the area eventually developed its own problems. The flats themselves are on today's hit list. The tower of St Michael's Parish Church can be seen on the horizon; below and to the left is the Castle Shoe Company building. Christ Church, which saw its official opening on Christmas Day in 1775, is further towards the right. The building of the church was paid for by Charles Roe, who cannily recovered some of his costs by offering plots for sale in the graveyard for family vaults and graves. You might just be able to pick out Berisford's Mill in Commercial Road; the mill was sadly destroyed by fire in the 1970s. Towards the top of the photograph on the right is the gas works on Gas Road, and a glimpse of the railway line can be seen nearby.

Right: A certain amount of controversy has long surrounded the Castle Inn just off Waters Green: is it the oldest pub in Macclesfield - or is it not? An Adsheads house at the time this photograph was taken the Castle is certainly one of the oldest, but having said that, a directory dating from the 1790s does not list the pub, though it existed in 1804, when it had a brewhouse. The 'period' frontage, though it certainly adds to the character of this well-known and popular watering-hole, is of course a modern addition. The Castle was privately owned until 1875, when Stockport brewers, Joseph Worrall (later taken over by Wilsons), acquired it. Twenty years later the then tenant Joshua Denton bought the Castle for £1,000 - a very large sum of money in those days.

The Castle is interesting in that it is one of those establishments whose name can actually be traced back to its origins. The pub undoubtedly owes its name to a mansion house with a castellated roof that stood adjacent to nearby Backwallgate, itself dating back to the fourteenth century when it was built by John de Macclesfield. The Castle continues to provide Maxonians with a pint or three of their favourite liquid refreshment.

This glimpse back in time shows us Macclesfield Market as it once was, full of life and with a character of its very own, and many local housewives, who love a bargain as much as anyone else, would have made a beeline for this spot in the old days. The well-stocked fruit stall in the photograph would have been the first port of call for many, where a good selection of apples, pears, oranges, grapefruit and bananas was on offer. The prices charged by street traders have traditionally been a few coppers cheaper than the larger shops would charge. Next to the greengrocer's stall is a pet shop, complete with bird cage. Products

for pets of every kind could be bought here; dog chews, doggy vitamins, collars, leads, and rabbit and guinea pig food. Note the sign in front advertising dog coats.

Forming a backdrop to the scene are the Town Hall, the police station, now of course situated in Brunswick Street, and the Parish Church. Will the tower of St Michael and All Angels ever preside over a similar scene in Market Place, one wonders? Many Maxonians believe that the market belongs in the traditional place that after all bears its name.... Watch this space!

Left: A very peaceful view of Park Green; though the exact date of the photograph is not known, it probably dates back to the early 1950s. There is little traffic about to worry pedestrians; even towards the end of the 1940s the effects of the war were still being felt, and certain goods remained in short supply. This included the motor car, as new cars were being exported as fast as they came off the production line. Though Britain still had a long way to go before post-war prosperity became a reality (a car was an unattainable dream for the average family), there were still a large number of mostly pre-war cars about.

This was a pleasant sunny day, as we can see by the white blinds above every shop in the row of businesses that occupied the Macclesfield Equitable and Provident Co-operative Society building. Spearings, Macc's well-known butcher's shop, is still there. On the far left of the photograph is the fine Victorian Gothic Congregational church, now the United Reform. Nearby is the site of Depot Mill, one of the town's very first silk mills; it was later demolished and a modern office block now stands there.

Above: This lovely old photograph of Macclesfield as it was, some time in the 1930s at a guess, gives us a nostalgic trip along Park Lane. Here we can revisit in imagination the shops that were familiar to Maxonians of yesteryear. The windows of Hollands' chemists shop were rather dull compared with those of today, that sparkle with jewellery, hair ornaments and cosmetics. This was the place to go, however, not only to have your doctor's medicines dispensed but to buy the popular home remedies that had stood the test of time: castor oil, ipecacuanha, camphorated oil, Indian Brandee and Fennings fever powders. Next door, Lyons Drapers sold everything from clothing to hearthrugs; note the rugs and carpets hung outside the shop. J B Jackson, optician and jeweller, came next, with Speakman's further along towards Old Park Lane, as this section of road is locally known. Hovis bread, advertised on a hoarding in the background, has been known in the area for many years; their flour was first produced at the Hovis mill in Union Road in 1885. Interestingly, the name Hovis (the winner of a competition to decide on a name for the bread) is a contraction of the Latin 'hominus vis' - 'the strength of man'.

There was little traffic about in Park Green when this peaceful scene was captured on camera; the street lamp and the designs of the cars standing at the kerb would suggest that it was taken sometime in the late 1950s. The contrasting designs of the cars are interesting; the somewhat austere lines typical of earlier decades, and the lighter, sleeker lines that developed in the post-war years, when colour was introduced into motor car design. The Ford Popular was an affordable little vehicle, and some readers may perhaps remember it with fondness as their very first car. Do you remember the strange layout of the gears, with reverse where first gear would be on other cars? And the hand-brake under the dashboard? And the vacuum wipers that gave up when you put your foot down and flogged away like mad when you eased off the accelerator?

At that time, the impressive building we now know as the United Reform Church would have been the Macclesfield Congregational church; the union was formed in 1972, when the Congregationalists and Presbyterians came together to form the United Reform Church. Built in 1877, the church was built on the site of the old Pickford Eyes Farm.

Above: This wonderfully evocative photograph of the Electricity Showrooms in Mill Street (where it remained until it moved around the corner in the 1970s) is filled with reminders of the domestic life of our mothers and grandmothers. The windows are packed with electrical gadgets that were up-to-the-minute in their day; the delightful electric kettles, for example, that resembled copper kettles in appearance; and do you remember those circular electric fires that had the element sticking up in the middle? They came in handy to warm up a cold room while you were waiting for Dad to light the coal fire with firelighters, a wigwam of sticks, a few coals - and often a shovel standing in front draped with newspaper to draw the fire! Note the old vacuum cleaner with its cloth bag (was this a Hoover?) - it's surprising how many of these machines survive, and still in working order! The cloth bag itself had to be removed and emptied: no disposable paper bags in those days! At the rear of one of the windows stands an electric oven, the pride and joy of many housewives of the day, though waiting for those solid metal plates to heat up and boil a pan of water could be compared to the joys of watching a plank warp.

Do you remember when....?

Memories. We all have them; some good, some bad, but our memories of the town we grew up in are usually tucked away in a very special place in our minds. The best are usually connected with our childhood and youth, when we longed to be grown up and paid no attention to adults who told us to enjoy our youth, as these were the best years of our lives. We look back now and realise that they were right.

We remember crowding into the Saturday matinee at the Picturedrome or the Majestic with our mates to throw bits of rubbish around and watch the cliffhanger serial that left its heroine, pale-faced but still beautiful, tied to the railway line for a whole nailbiting week. And what about those wonderful afternoons when we shouted ourselves hoarse for the Silkmen? We remember Mike Black's coffee bar in Queen Victoria Street, dancing the night away at the El Rio, and our very first pint at the Brewer's Arms - or was it the Bate Hall?

So many memories. And so many changes. Macclesfield during the war, when thousands of evacuees descended on the town; Christmas Eve 1940, when bombs killed three at Lower Grotto Farm at Over Peover; the Dakota that crashed at Bosley in December 1944 killing nine US airmen. Macclesfield in later years when the Central station, The Angel pub, the Infirmary, the Stanley Hall, and whole streets of cosy terraced houses all disappeared in the name of progress.

And we can think of sweeping changes of a different kind, when those first self-serve stores opened in the 1960s. Remember them? How strange it felt at first to help ourselves from the goods on display on the shelves - it was almost like stealing! Those small self-service shops led quickly to the opening of the larger super-markets such as Sainsbury's and Tesco's - and eventually resulted in the demise of many of Macclesfield's corner shops and small grocers. We remember, also, the silk mills, where our parents and grandparents worked - an industry that was virtually destroyed by the advent of man-made fibres and synthetics.

Macclesfield, however, not only survived but prospered. Though the town is no longer the Silk Capital of Britain, Maxonians nevertheless have a history to be proud of - and a great future to look forward to, into the new millennium and beyond.

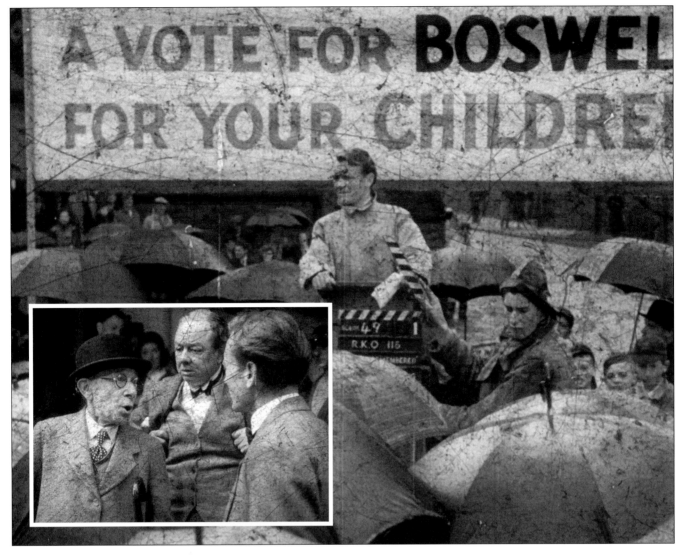

This page: Even the fire brigade lent their services when the Hollywood film company RKO descended on Macclesfield to shoot the film 'So Well Remembered' - an event that drew Maxonians together as little else before or since. A mere handful of professional actors had roles in the film, while as these stills show, hundreds of Macclesfield residents took part.

Based on a book of the same name by the author of 'Lost Horizon', the film starred John Mills, Patricia Roc and Leslie Howard. The film was set in a ficti-tious northern mill town, and John Mills (later Sir John Mills) played the role of a 'local boy made good', with Patricia Roc as his girl friend. His character eventually became MP for the town, and the scene that portrays him making his election speech (from the library, which was used as a town hall) called for bad weather and heavy rain. Being a fine day, the necessary rain was provided by the hoses of the local fire brigade.

The northern premier was held at the Macclesfield Majestic, which saw packed houses night after night. It must have been fascinating for the local people to view themselves, their families, friends and neighbours on the silver screen along with famous actors. And seeing the local streets and countryside on screen was quite an experience, too, as all the locations were quite dislocated and had no connection with each other. Demand for the film continued, and after a few weeks it was shown at the Picture Drome, again to full houses.

In the early 1980s a one-off showing for charity was arranged by Peter Higginbotham, director of the Majestic, local headmaster Keith Yearsley, and Doug Pickford, who was then editor of the Macclesfield Express. Tickets were like gold dust.

What a shame the film has never been shown on television or been made available on video.

Above: A busy shopping day in Chestergate, when it was normal to see traffic making its way along the narrow street. A delivery van advertises B & B Champion Bread; and is that a Wolseley 1500 further along? Pedestrianised in 1988, Chestergate has seen many changes over the years, notably the building of the Grosvenor Shopping Centre. Only this well-known view of the Town Hall never seems to change - though the market stalls in front of it in Market Place are now no longer there. Remember Beverly's Wines and Spirits on the right of the photograph? And Whittakers camera shop? Ilford films are advertised outside; whenever did Ilford films disappear from our shops? John Douglas, gents outfitters, occupies the same shop today, on the corner of the new shopping precinct. Further along is the Copper Kettle. The cafe to bring a host of memories flooding back, however, is the UCP Restaurant on the left of Chestergate. Its full title 'United Cattle Products Restaurant' is hardly one to tempt many of today's finicky eaters, but older readers will surely remember it, and the snack bar on the ground floor - and those delicious meals of tripe, pigs' trotters, black pudding, brawn and oxtail that could be had there.

Right: A wonderfully nostalgic glimpse back 60 years or so at Bradleys outfitters, who catered for the clothing needs of the well-dressed Macclesfield gentleman for many years. Suits and jackets both formal and informal, shirts and ties for every occasion - and certain more intimate items of a gentleman's underwear were all stocked by the well-known Chestergate store. In later years the Chestergate entrance to the Grosvenor Shopping Centre was to be situated right opposite Bradleys, which changed hands in the late 1960s. To the left is Byram's Café, the scene of many a pleasant lunchtime meeting with friends, while still further along Chestergate to the left lies the ancient hostelry, the Bate Hall Hotel. The sixteenth-century building's claim to fame was that Oliver Cromwell is believed to have stayed there in the days when it belonged to the Stopfords, a prominent local Roundhead family. It was turned into an inn sometime in the eighteenth century.

The well-known furniture store Rileys lay off-picture to the right, and many a Macclesfield couple set up home with dining tables, chairs, sideboards and three-piece suites from Rileys. The store is, of course, now long gone.

Below: An almost final look at Mill Street as it was in the 1960s, and a top of the range Vauxhall saloon is the only sign of life in the street that once buzzed with life. We can see that many of the shops have already been acquired prior to demolition; the Home & Colonial looks very forlorn with its paper-covered window. Many will remember shopping here in the 'old days' which truth to tell do not seem so long past. The Home & Colonial might have been the first port of call for the housewife shopping for the family, filling her capacious shopping bag with fruit and vegetables and a few canned goods. A visit to W & G Burdin further along would provide her with more groceries, while her Sunday roast of pork, beef or lamb were purchased next door. Children must have been fascinated by the giant key hanging prominently outside the ironmongers, Charles A Day & Co; in their imagination this could have been the key to the giant's castle (he of the beanstalk fame).

Today, of course, though the buildings are new and the road is pedestrianised, Mill Street is vibrant with life once again, with Marks & Spencer, Waterstones and W H Smith occupying these positions.

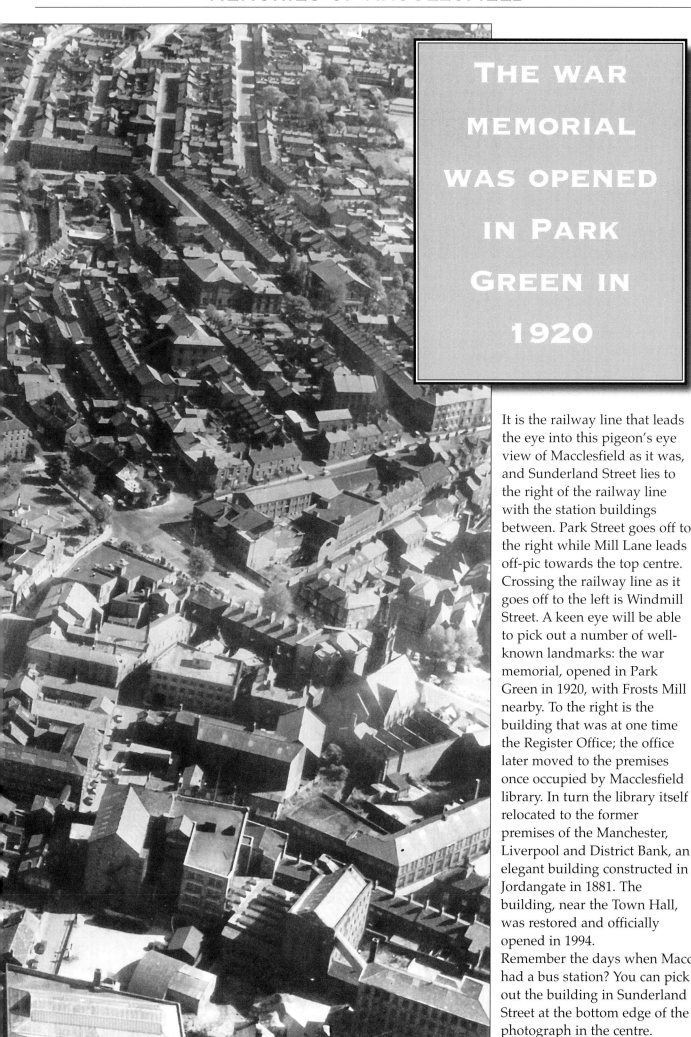

THE WAR MEMORIAL WAS OPENED IN PARK GREEN IN 1920

It is the railway line that leads the eye into this pigeon's eye view of Macclesfield as it was, and Sunderland Street lies to the right of the railway line with the station buildings between. Park Street goes off to the right while Mill Lane leads off-pic towards the top centre. Crossing the railway line as it goes off to the left is Windmill Street. A keen eye will be able to pick out a number of well-known landmarks: the war memorial, opened in Park Green in 1920, with Frosts Mill nearby. To the right is the building that was at one time the Register Office; the office later moved to the premises once occupied by Macclesfield library. In turn the library itself relocated to the former premises of the Manchester, Liverpool and District Bank, an elegant building constructed in Jordangate in 1881. The building, near the Town Hall, was restored and officially opened in 1994.

Remember the days when Macc had a bus station? You can pick out the building in Sunderland Street at the bottom edge of the photograph in the centre.

The town of Macclesfield lies far below us like a 3-dimensional map, and like a step back in time jogs our memories of what things were like before modernisation swept away many of the buildings we knew. On the left of the photograph is Ryles Pool and South Park, which has seen many occasions in its day, from the gentle pleasures of the Sunday afternoon brass band playing from its bandstand to the choosing of the Silk Queen at the Macclesfield Carnival. The impressive Heritage Centre, originally the Macclesfield Sunday School, lies towards the top and to the right of the photograph. Nearby to the right you might just pick out the Majestic Cinema - the last of Macclesfield's cinemas - which closed in 1997. A short distance below is the Depot Mill, now demolished. Silk House now occupies the site. To the right of Depot Mill is the El Rio Dance Hall, whose management brought the Fab Four to Macclesfield on January 26th 1963 for the Beatles' only concert in the town. A mere five shillings would have secured you a ticket for the sensational event! You might also recognise the old bus station, the cenotaph and Frost's Mill, while the London-Manchester railway line curves across the bottom right side of the picture.

On the move

Below: It's a long time since North Western buses were seen around the town in their smart red and cream livery. These two buses, one with Park Royal School on its destination blind, are standing in the bus station in Sunderland Street - today part of Macclesfield's largest garage company, J J Cookson's premises. This post-war photograph dates from the late 1940s or early 1950s, when bus operators were beginning to recover from the effects of the war - a tough time for them in many different ways. Spare parts were as rare as hens' teeth, and many buses were in urgent need of maintenance - yet at the same time there was an increased demand for public transport because of petrol rationing. Many members of staff enlisted in the services and women stepped in as drivers and conductresses. The blackout too caused problems, and drivers had to learn to 'feel' their way around the streets, while inside the lights were so dim that the unfortunate conductresses scarcely knew whether they were being given a halfpenny or a shilling!

Right: This seemingly unremarkable photograph, probably taken in the early 1930s, raises as many questions as it answers. Why is this lovely old North Western bus in the car park outside the old Central Station instead of in the nearby bus station where it would normally be? Obviously a special group of people has been picked up; passengers looking out of the windows smile for the camera, and the conductor poses in the doorway, proud of his charge that day. The occasion merits the attendance of Inspector Smith (whose brother Harold, who worked for the local newspaper, was well known in the town). According to the destination on the blind, the bus is bound for Bollington. Note the drop-down passenger windows, and the driver's window that was hinged to open, allowing lots of fresh air to circulate around the bus.

The scene will no doubt bring back fond memories, not just of the old North Western buses but of Central Station and the bus depot in Sunderland Street, of friends met, journeys made - and buses and trains missed!

Both pictures: The nostalgia is all there: the old steam engine with its noisy clatter and unexpected hisses of steam approaches Central Station from Manchester on the LMS line. All that is needed is a couple of train-spotting boys busily scribbling engine numbers in their notebooks. Whatever happened to this harmless hobby? The advent of television, video and computer games signalled the demise of many such innocent pastimes, and many of today's railway enthusiasts are in their fifties or sixties. But steam was doomed, and though they were far quieter and not a little cleaner owing to the absence of soot, the diesel and electric trains that were introduced across the country in the mid-1950s definitely lacked the character of the old steam engine. This diesel train (below), passing under Beech Lane Bridge has

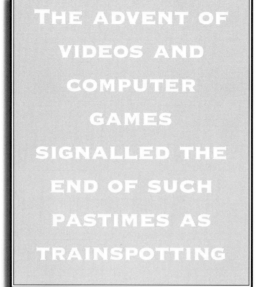

THE ADVENT OF VIDEOS AND COMPUTER GAMES SIGNALLED THE END OF SUCH PASTIMES AS TRAINSPOTTING

'Macclesfield Hibel Road' on its destination blind, though the days of Hibel Road Station were in fact numbered. It was closed down in 1960.

Macclesfield has had a railway service since 1845, when the London and North Western Railway constructed a temporary station. Hibel Road Station replaced it four years later.

There have been a number of fingers in the pies of Macclesfield's railway service; the North Staffordshire Railway began running a service to Congleton and Leek in 1849, and the Macclesfield, Bollington and Marple Railway opened Macclesfield Central Station in 1873. Part of the Bollington and Marple line, which closed in 1970, was utilised for the Silk Road. Today Hibel Road Station is the site of the Tesco superstore.

Above: A scene that along with many other well-known landmarks in the town is now gone for ever, but many readers will no doubt still remember Ray's mineral water factory. Presided over by the tower of Christ Church the staff have positioned their vans strategically for this formal photograph, and stand proudly beside their vehicles to smile for the camera. The firm's cat is determined to get in on the act too, and Tiddles has cosily settled down on the probably warm bonnet of the centre vehicle. Was the photograph taken to mark a particular occasion, we wonder, or did the boss one day suddenly say, 'I know - let's have our picture taken'? It's impossible to know, but interesting to speculate....

The mineral water works buildings were eventually demolished and turned into a car park for Moss and Smith. Three times every week the car park becomes a hive of activity when market traders take over and set up their colourful stalls. If campaigners have their way, however, the situation could change in the future and the market be returned to its original home in Market Place.

Right: What a crash that must have been! The devastation caused in Jordangate when this vehicle - thought to be a fire engine - collided with the tobacconist-cum-newsagent's frontage and overturned in September 1950 almost resembles a scene from the wartime blitz. Little remained of the shop doorway and the adjoining wall, and a number of the windows appears to be shattered. Heavy lifting gear has been brought in to remove the vehicle, while in the background a small group of spectators, attracted by the drama, has gathered to watch as the fire engine is set back on its wheels and taken away. The young boy is obviously enjoying the free show, as virtually every boy in the country would, but the much younger little girls (his sisters perhaps?) seem to be very unhappy about the whole incident, and cling to each other's hands for comfort while Mum reassures them that everything is really OK. Chatting with one of the neighbours who had a lucky escape is Times reporter Philip Murray in the trilby hat and coat. A first hand account of the incident is forthcoming, no doubt.

At leisure

THE WATERS GREEN FAIR ALWAYS HAD AN ATMOSPHERE THAT HAD TO BE EXPERIENCED TO BE APPRECIATED

Do you remember, as a child or teenager, those wonderful evenings you spent at Waters Green fair? This lovely photograph will no doubt bring back many memories of good times had long ago. Though we have no accurate date for the picture, this view was certainly captured some time during the late 1950s.

The Waters Green fair has always had an atmosphere of its very own that has to be experienced to be appreciated, and older readers will perhaps believe that this was more true in their youth. The whirr and hum of the rides, the loud beat of the music, several different tunes fighting with each other for attention, the shouts of the man who bravely volunteered to guess your weight, the squeals of the girls as they rose to the top of the big wheel. And the food! The shocking pink candy floss that was sold from booths and was spun around a stick while you waited, the toffee apples, dark red and shining as if they had been varnished, the paper bags of crunchy brandy snap and the ice cream, in tubs, cornets or wafers. All very thrilling stuff, and calculated to send any child home tired and satisfied at the end of a wonderful day out.

St Paul's church stands benignly in the background as if bestowing its blessing on this tranquil Sunday scene in Macclesfield. It was the 1950s, and Step Hill Gardens - known locally as Sparrow Park - had recently been renovated. This was the first Sunday after the reopening of the gardens, and on that warm and sunny day large numbers of people turned out to spend an hour or so among its walks and flower beds. Those were the days when the simple pleasures of a stroll in the park or a ramble through the countryside were still appreciated. Though a couple of cars are parked near the gardens, in actual fact few families had cars back then, and the custom of taking the children to theme parks, or spending a day in out-of-town shopping centres was still in the distant future. Though tame by today's pleasure-loving generation, a walk in Step Hill Gardens, so conveniently placed behind the Borough Council municipal offices, remained a popular pastime.

Note the length of the dresses worn by the ladies in the photograph; flared or gathered skirts which reached at least mid-calf were typical of the 1950s fashions which were a direct reaction against the skimpy wartime utility clothing.

One of these outings was made by the all-male staff of Young & Co Builders and/or C J Dale & Son Decorators; possibly both firms went together, as a prominently placed notice on the double gateway says 'Closed for annual outing'. Can we assume that following the joys of Blackpool (or some similar seaside destination) there would be a few headaches among the workforce the following morning?

Interestingly, all the children in the large crowd in the older photograph seem to be labelled in case they wandered off and got lost. Probably a wise move given the unpredictability of the average six-year-old. Who these children were and where they were going has been lost in the mists of time, but their eager smiles and waves to the camera leave us in no doubt that this was going to be a red letter day in their young lives. Their two coaches wait in the background for them to board.

Both pages: A coat and some headgear in case it rains, a light summer frock, a white handbag and a pair of sandals in case of warm sunshine - the happy day-trippers in these nostalgic photographs were ready to face anything. If it rained, why worry? Amusement arcades, funfairs, shops and local pubs all presented a welcome change from the realities of working life.

Where the trippers in these groups were bound we do not know, but there is scarcely a face that doesn't appear to be looking forward to their day out.

Everyone loves a day trip, and the delights of Blackpool topped the popularity charts with local people, especially those who could not afford to get away for a fortnight's holiday. The occasional day trip to Blackpool, New Brighton, Llandudno or Rhyl, or a visit to Buxton was eagerly anticipated.

Below: Ernest Farrar, who kept Adshead's off licence shop, was obviously quite a character in the district. It was Ernest who led the Lower Hurdsfield coronation procession back in 1953, and he was backed up by crowds of fun loving locals who donned costumes and carried appropriate props for the occasion. The event was clearly 'anything for a laugh', and the lady to the right of the photograph would have raised many a titter from spectators as she waved her chamber pot (known to many as a 'guzunder'; for the benefit of younger readers who from birth have lived in homes with indoor toilets we include the explanation that the item in question 'guzunder' the bed!). The 'chamber full of blooms' joke is emphasised by the sign she carries: 'Won't you buy my pretty flowers'.

Macclesfield put her back into the country-wide party held to celebrate the coronation, and even the sedately pillared frontage of the Town Hall was bedecked with garlands, flags, crowns and banners - and a huge sign that spelled out the town's loyalty with the message 'Long live the Queen'.

Right: It was the midsummer Barnaby annual holiday, and this crowd of happy holidaymakers were bound for Blackpool. The date given for this photograph is 24th June 1950, though judging by the coats, scarves, hats and stout shoes that are in evidence a considerable increase in the temperature would be needed before these Macclesfield folk would be able to do much in the way of deckchair sitting. At least it wasn't raining!

There appear to be few children waiting for the coach, and the little chap in front looks rather lonely. No doubt he would find many play-mates once their destination was reached - there has always been plenty to do at Blackpool. First of all the beach beckoned, and weather permitting children with buckets and spades would make a beeline along the promenade and on to the sand to build castles and dig moats that would fill with water as the tide came in. Parents would lounge in a deck chair nearby where they could keep an eye on what the children were doing. Another day they might walk on one of the piers, take a tram ride, see a show at the Winter Gardens, visit the aquarium and the zoo in Blackpool Tower, or even take the thrilling ride to the very top.

Both pictures: Marching bands were a feature of the Macclesfield Carnival, and the swinging, foot-stomping Heatherbells provided plenty of music for the onlookers in the watching crowds to tap their feet to. And you didn't need to be an expert on the trumpet or the saxophone to play in this jazz band - all you needed was a kazoo, the ability to hum in tune, and a sense of rhythm. Look at all those marching feet - each one completely in step! The Heatherbells were just one of the many bands who took part in the carnival parade; each of the silk mills in the

town formed their own band of marchers and musicians.

With the children at the front (above right) where they could obtain a ringside view of the carnival parade, Maxonians lined the pavements along the entire route at least three deep. The fashions worn by the spectators are typical of the elegant days of the 1930s, when few people - men as well as women and children - went out without a hat. At least one gentleman in this crowd, however, has defied convention and gone out bareheaded; perhaps that day was a particularly warm one! The procession passes along Cumberland Street and past the tree-lined grounds of Macclesfield Infirmary, to which all the funds brought in by the collectors that day were donated. The Infirmary was later demolished and a branch of Sainsbury's supermarket chain now occupies the site.

Above: Readers with long memories will immediately recognise the young woman in this photograph as Jean Alexander, who back in the late 1940s was a member of the Macclesfield Adelphi Players. The theatre-goers of the day will readily acknowledge that Jean had already established herself as an able actress long before she joined the cast of 'Coronation Street' as Hilda Ogden, the role which was to bring her country-wide fame.

The Adelphi Players were originally an offshoot of a group of actors who entertained the hundreds of Londoners sheltering in the underground during the Blitz. In 1947 the travelling repertory company made their base in Macclesfield, playing at the Brocklehurst Memorial Hall in Queen Victoria Street. Their usual programme was to play for a week at their home theatre, then spend two to three weeks on tour around the neighbouring towns. Brocklehurst Memorial Hall, also known as the Liberal Club, was in the 1960s opened as the El Rio dance hall, with 'Barmy Barry' as its DJ. Many of the big names in the pop world appeared at the El Rio - including The Beatles.

THE ADELPHI PLAYERS WERE ORIGINALLY AN OFFSHOOT OF A GROUP OF ACTORS WHO ENTERTAINED DURING THE BLITZ

Though the pattern of these silk costumes is reminiscent of the flamboyant designs of the 1970s, the wardrobe worn by the marchers in this photograph belongs to a much earlier decade - the 1930s. Passing the end of Waterloo Street is the 'Prize' jazz band of Frost & Sons, whose mill was in Park Green. Obviously winners in a previous year's carnival parade, these young people appear to be full of confidence. Did they pip the other bands to the post on this occasion as well? we have to

wonder. The banner on the float in the background informs spectators along the route of the carnival procession that not only was the silk for these wonderful costumes woven by Macclesfield mill BWA Ltd (Brocklehurst, Whiston Amalgamated) but they were also made up there. The sharp-eyed may be able to spot an entertainer on stilts in the background to the right of the banner; the children along the route would have found this tall top-hatted man, probably a fundraiser, fascinating.

Left: Macclesfield held their very own coronation processions in the 1930s carnival parades and though this Silk Queen's coach is not quite as grand as Queen Elizabeth's golden State Coach of June 1953, the smile on her face and on those of her attendants is every bit as genuine. The pageantry of the Queen's coronation is well-remembered by a nation who viewed it on television. The sight of the new queen being anointed with oil and having the crown placed upon her head is one which few can forget. Many are not aware that the Queen's coronation dress was itself symbolic, being embroidered with the emblems of the Dominions - India, Canada, New Zealand and Australia. When the ceremony was over, the Queen rode back to the palace in her golden coach, wearing the crown and carrying the orb and sceptre. Unlike her father King George VI, the young and pretty new queen had begun her training for the throne early, when Edward VIII's abdication in 1936 made her the heir presumptive to the throne. She was only 14 years old when as Princess Elizabeth she broadcast messages of encouragement to the children of war-torn Britain, and as the war progressed she gradually took on more and more public duties.

Above: The Beach Brigade Prize Jazz Band - and every one of their delightful costumes was made from silk produced in Macclesfield. These marchers in the grand Carnival Parade were from one of the local mills. Every mill in the town entered not only their jazz bands but decorated floats and a bevy of silk princesses, every one hoping to be chosen as the year's Silk Queen. Take note of the little cutie on the far right of the photograph. Determined to enter into the spirit of things and dress up for the occasion, the tiny tot is fixing a shiny star into her hair.

Readers may recognise the streets and houses in this photograph - the parade is passing the end of Waterloo Street - though they no longer exist today, having been demolished to make way for the Victoria Park flats development. The sharp-eyed will notice the advertisement on a wall in the background for Oxade, a drink which could have been popular at the time but today taxes our memories. Despite the sound of its name this drink has nothing to do with Oxo; further investigation reveals that Oxade was actually a soft drink.

At work

IN THE 1930S A

JOINT OF PORK

WOULD COST

YOU MORE THAN

A SIMILAR JOINT

OF BEEF

There were few vegetarians around in the 1930s; Watson's butcher's shop in Stanley Street was only one of many in the town, and Charley Watson - seen standing in the shop doorway - was justifiably proud of his fine display of meat and his special offers. Bill Bayley on the left was obviously Charley's right hand man, while young apprentice Jack Sutton on the right was still learning the trade. The printed signs are fascinating; the grand sum of 1/6d would secure you a large rabbit (people ate more of them then) and a pound of beef or mutton - and a pound of carrots was thrown in for good measure. Even in the 1930s 1/6d - seven and a half pence in today's coinage - was clearly considered a bargain. A cut of prime pork could be had for between tenpence and a shilling a pound, while interestingly beef was considerably cheaper at between fourpence and tenpence. This remarkable glimpse back through time was captured in 1934; with his life and career before him, young Jack Sutton chose not to stay in the butchering business. He later worked for plastics firm Ferodo, where he made a name for himself as the inventor of the original plastic football, now used worldwide today.

Left: Who in the Silk Capital needs a history lesson about Macclesfield's rich history in the silk weaving industry? It is on silk, after all, that the town's reputation as the principal producer in the area was built, and although the industry eventually declined, especially after the second world war, much still remains to remind us of the days when 10,000 local people worked in some aspect of silk production. A few textile producers survived, however, and this atmospheric old photograph was taken in Josiah Smales' silk mill in George Street, though the date is unknown. Mrs Mary Bradbury can be seen in the foreground, with Mrs Rachel Bradbury working at the next loom. George Newton, a weaver, is standing in the background.
It is to the town's credit that our fascinating heritage in silk throwing, dyeing and weaving has been preserved in the silk museum, part of the Heritage Centre, and at Paradise Mill in Park Lane, where our children and grandchildren as well as Macc's many visitors, can see the processes for themselves and find out how so many old Maxonians made their living long ago.

Above: This ingenious 'float', with a couple of pylons connected by electric cables, was entered in the Macclesfield Carnival by the Electricity Board during the 1930s. Many homes were still lit by gas as late as the 1940s, so at the time this photograph was taken electric lighting was still a novelty to many. According to the sign on this vehicle, electricity could be had 'at the touch of the magic switch', and you can probably recognise the picture of a finger pressing a switch on a display board in front of the van. The vehicle itself ran on electricity , and was advertised as 'the cheapest transport for tradesmen'. An address and telephone number was given to encourage people to ask for full particulars of the electric vehicles.
The young men pictured with the van are staff from Electric House in Mill Street. The electricity showroom in Mill Street (readers may remember the cafe above) was there until the 1970s. It relocated to premises around the corner, where it remains today.

Above: The rather nice bungalows being built here in Ivy Road on the Weston Estate in 1949 formed part of Macclesfield's answer to the lack of sufficient housing that by the mid 1940s was becoming a real problem. It was judged that part of the solution lay in demolishing many of the older properties in the town, and Commercial Road and the surrounding streets were swept away, and soul-less new council flats and houses were built to replace them. Many of the old Commercial Road residents were rehoused in these

bungalows. The Ivy Road project made full use of the workers at their disposal, and these young apprentices were employed on site. A number of budding joiners, builders and plumbers are pictured here as they put their talents into learning a useful trade. Interestingly, many of the concrete roads on the Weston Estate were laid by German prisoners-of-war. The building of the Weston Estate was initiated by Sir Garfield Weston, a former Macclesfield MP and a member of the Weston family, the well-known confectioner who manufacture the popular Wagon Wheels biscuits.

Above right: The badges on the uniforms tells us that these were members of the National Fire Service, an organisation that did much vital work across the country during the second world war. At least one prominent member of the community is pictured here: Mr Eric Burgess of the family company Burgess

Engineering is sixth from the left. Mr Burgess was an ardent follower of Macclesfield FC, and in later life became well known as a Rotarian.

During the war the National Fire Service took control of all civic fire brigades, and women as well as men worked for the NFS. Many women acted as fire watchers; on occasions incendiaries had fallen into unattended office blocks and factories and started fires - a two-hour bombing raid on London just after Christmas in 1940 started a total of 1,500 fires, many of them burning unchecked in city centre properties. After that, firewatching became a compulsory duty, and all men between 16 and 60 were called on to organise a fire-watching rota. Later on women between 20 and 45 joined them. The second world war called for volunteers of both sexes to fulfil all kinds of duties, and Macclesfield, along with the rest of Britain, pulled their weight.

Below: All ready for a long day's fundraising for their hospital, these nurses from Macclesfield Infirmary pose with their collecting boxes for the camera; the words on their boxes reads 'Please patronise Carnival effort for the Infirmary'. The event was the Macclesfield Carnival, some time in the 1930s (though the exact date is not known), and hundreds of townspeople turned out to watch the grand parade of ingeniously decorated floats and the magnificently-dressed hopeful Silk Queens and their princesses, as they passed through the streets of the town towards South Park, where the new Silk Queen was elected and crowned. Hundreds of women in the town would no doubt have been busy at their sewing machines for many weeks, running up the scores of different costumes and the elaborate decorations for the floats. The eager nurses in this photograph would have done a lot of box-rattling during the day as they passed among the good-natured crowds, expecting them to dig deep in their pockets and support their own hospital.

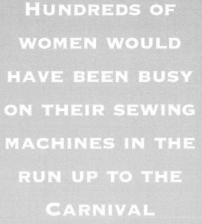

HUNDREDS OF WOMEN WOULD HAVE BEEN BUSY ON THEIR SEWING MACHINES IN THE RUN UP TO THE CARNIVAL

Left: It was 1967, and the Macclesfield rotary press has just finished producing the latest edition of the County Express; members of staff are carefully checking copies of the paper before distribution. The press was kept busy for much of the week - as well as the Macclesfield paper the County Express, the Sale and Altrincham newspapers and a number of others in the South Manchester area were all printed here. The staff were mostly local people who produced the weekly papers.

The rotary press itself had a colourful history, and would probably have had many a tale to tell. Before being acquired by the Macclesfield printing works it had produced the rather more racy events reported in the News of the World. In its early years the press had been steam-driven, then was converted to run on electricity.

The printing works was demolished when plans to build the Grosvenor Shopping Centre were put into operation, and the quiet chatter of electric tills at Boots the Chemist has now replaced the noisy clatter of printing presses.

Above: Almost - but not quite - caught on camera is overlooker Jim Statham, pictured with the matrix machines at the printing works of the Macclesfield County Express. Those who like to know what machines are for might like to know that the matrix machines produced a papier maché impression of each of the newspaper's pages - an essential part of the printing process. Readers may remember the days when the building shared by the Macclesfield Press and the Macclesfield County Express printing works fronted on to Castle Street, with the rear of the building in Stanley Street. At that time Macclesfield and the surrounding towns were rich in publications, all of which were produced and sent on their way from this printing works. The selection of newspapers, along with the building, are now part of the town's history. Over the years the different papers amalgamated to become the Macclesfield Express, today the only local paper you can buy over the counter from a newsagent. The everyday events of the town have been covered by a local newspaper since 1811, when the Macclesfield Courier was printed from premises in Market Place.

Providing shelter from the storm

For decades, countless homes have been able to keep out rainwater and draughts thanks to Stormguard's innovative weatherproofing products. Stormguard is the tradename of a family business in Macclesfield which originated in 1810, and is known today as The Stormguard Group. In that year Mr Green and Mr Stringer established a machine shop on the corner of Catherine Street and Pierce Street, in a four-storey, brick-built former textile mill, constructed in about 1760. Its original tiny, cast iron window frames were still intact in 1978 when the building was sold for conversion into flats, and the stone foundations are still visible three feet above pavement level.

In this building, jobbing engineers Stringer and Green seem to have prospered. Growing industrialisation led to an increase in the number of local businesses who made use of their engineering services, and within the next decade, in 1816, a foundry was added in Pinfold Street. The two original foundry cranes were still in operation when this foundry closed in 1975; the larger has been left in position as an historic feature, and the smaller was donated to a museum in Newcastle upon Tyne.

In the first half of the 19th century a Bollington millowner, Mr Swindells, employed a local man called Joseph Watts as works manager. Joseph Watts fell in love with and married his employer's daughter Mary, and it was this young couple's son, Martin, who later married Mr Green's daughter Anne, and in 1847 bought the business from his father-in-law for the sum of £1600.

An Edwardian brass name plate proudly advertised 'Martin H. Watts - Engineer - Brass and Iron Founder - Steam Engines - Pumps - Pulleys and Shafting - Rope Driving - Wheel Gearing - Sound Castings Light and Heavy'.

Martin Watts was principally occupied by the manufacture and repair of machinery for the textile mills, such as steam engines and boilers. One of Watts' own steam engines was the Regent, which was manufactured towards the end of the century and named after the Pinfold Street foundry.

Martin and Anne Watts' son Martin Henry took the business over in 1878 after his father's death, and continued along the same lines, fabricating cast iron street gas lamps and Macclesfield cast iron door sill thresholds which became known as the Macclesfield Door Sill, and original sills are still in place today in some homes in Mount Pleasant along the Prestbury Road - installed about 1880.

Martin Henry Watts was succeeded as the owner of the Watts Engineering business by his son Percy in 1924. Percy had graduated from Manchester University with a first class Honours degree in Mathematics, and during the first world

Above: Steam engine made by Watts in the late 1800s.
Left: The brass name plate for Watts Engineers.

war had been a junior officer on the trench artillery guns. He ran the family business from the time of his father's death in 1924 until his own sudden death, from a heart attack, in November 1959. During this period the firm's products, besides munition parts manufactured during the second world war, included machinery for his father-in-law's dyeworks in Waller Street, a 30 foot paper combiner for the Slaters' Card Factory, and the original Hovis cookers for the first Hovis Mill in Brooke Street, Macclesfield. These huge cookers were used for baking the wheat germs, and the last one was made by Peter Allmand Smith in 1963 using the original foundry patterns.

During the 1930s and 1940s George Walley, one of the foundry workers, used to wheel a barrow round the streets of the town to pick up horse manure dropped by the many horses and carts used in those days. Horse manure was needed to mix with the sand and coal dust used to make hard baked sand cores necessary when making the sand moulded iron castings.

Unfortunately, during the late 1950s cast iron suddenly fell from favour as a material for industrial machinery and the business became severely run down; the total turnover during the first 10 months of 1959 did not exceed £10,000, and the

business's total assets, including the dilapidated workshop, amounted to some £3,000. The firm possessed no motor vehicle, and all materials were transported through the streets of Macclesfield by means of a two-wheeled hand cart.

Peter Allmand-Smith, Percy Watts' son-in-law (who was formerly a mining engineer), took over as manager in 1959, managing the business for his mother-in-law after Percy's sudden death, on a wage of £750 per annum plus any profit he could make. It was several years before any profits were accrued; during the first year he succeeded in increasing the business' turnover but still made an overall loss of £3000. Eventually there were sufficient funds to invest £50 in an A40 pick-up, then £200 in an old five-ton Ford truck (with a draughty, leaky cab and no heater) to carry the castings. None of Peter Allmand-Smith's 12 employees had a driving licence so he had to drive the Ford all over the country himself. It seems ironic that the man who was to devise the ultimate draught and rain excluding systems should have been exposed to so much draught and damp during his early days in the business.

In 1962 the pattern shop was re-opened to make patterns for the manufacture of fire bottom grate castings for local authorities' solid fuel fires which provided regular volume work until the Councils changed to smokeless fuel in 1967. The foundry then began to cast boat keels for the Hurley Boat Company through Avery's Foundry of Birmingham.

The firm also fabricated a large Stenter machine for a dyeworks in Nottingham in 1965;

Left: A page from a ledger dating from 1859.
Above: Inside the Regent Foundry machine shop in 1910 where castings were produced. The foundry still stands today in its original form.

this ambitious project took nine months to complete, and brought in a sum of £9,000.

Stormguard invested this money in devising a new version of the Macclesfield cast iron sill in extruded alloy, specifically designed to prevent rainwater and draughts from ingressing under external doors. He successfully marketed this to local author-ities, builders' merchants and ironmongers as the Stormguard Sill, and soon realised that there was a much more secure future for the firm in manufacturing and marketing its own goods than in doing jobbing work for other firms.

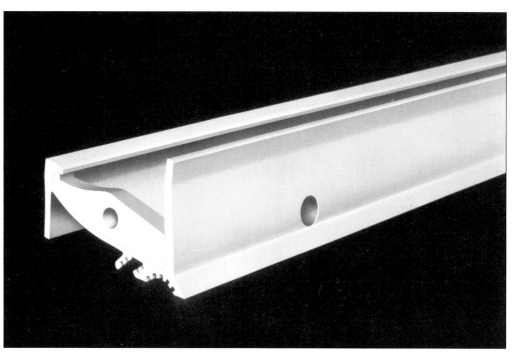

By 1969 Peter Allmand-Smith had developed the Slik range of domestic sliding door gear, designed to convert hinged doors into sliding doors, which sold 159,000 sets in the first year.

By that time the market for boat keels had dried up and in 1972 and the foundry was forced to close. The firm was well established as a manufacturer of new products such as door sills, door gear and draught excluders and door furniture. Innovations developed, such as a new

Above: The original design of Stormguard sill.
Below: A Stenter machine which was made by Watts in 1965 for the dyeing industry.

ADS (around the door strip) consisting of flexible rubber threaded into an extruded alloy carrier, Stormguard rain deflectors, spring loaded draught excluders, a draughtproof version of the Ball Race sliding door gear which became the market leader, and the Stormguard Lowline Superseal which consists of a centrally placed angled rubber strip on the floor of the stormguard with secondary drainholes, and this product proved to be a million-seller.

In 1965 Stormguard Group, in its infancy, had taken on its first salesman. By 1974 Stormguard was employing 17 salesmen covering the whole of the UK.

Above: An artist's drawing of the foundry yard in 1950.
Left: The foundry at Catherine Street, Macclesfield.

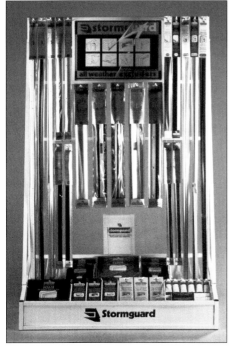

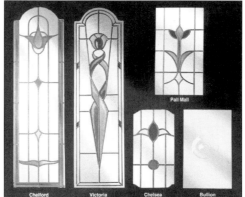

Five thousand accounts had been established and the firm possessed three important patents in speciality weather excluders. Stormguard were the market leaders in external threshold weather excluders and domestic sliding door gear. The firm's turnover had increased an average of 40% per year between 1965 and 1977 when the business was forced to move to Regency Mill to acquire more space.

At the present time the Stormguard Group own three substantial mills in Macclesfield and a non-ferrous foundry in Burnley.

its closure. This philanthropic action is entirely typical of the ethos of the company, reflecting as it does the strong Christian principles which are fundamental to all their dealings; indeed, Peter Allmand-Smith himself always attributes his business success not to his own innovation, enterprise and perseverance, but primarily to the constant intervention of Almighty God in all his affairs, to successfully counteract the foolishness of his own natural wisdom.

The name of the company was changed to Stormguard Sills in 1972 after the closure of the foundry, and Stormguard has gone from strength to strength. Stormguard is the UK's clear market-leader in quality weatherproofing for external household doors, and Stormguard products, which also include quality external doors and Olde English door furniture, are stocked by virtually all DIY and home improvement stores. Since 1988 exports to the USA have amounted to almost £2 million, and markets in Europe are currently being explored. The firm has increased from a total of 11 employees in 1959 turning over annually £10,000 to 130 employees in 1998 with a turnover of £8 million.

Acquisitions made by the company over the years include the purchase of Walters Brassworks, the non-ferrous foundry which made Olde English door furniture, together with its two and a half acres of building land in Burnley, in 1973; George's Mill, Chestergate, also in 1973; Regency Mill in 1976, and waste ground opposite for use as a car park in 1980, Paradise Mills in Old Park Lane in 1982, County Doors in 1984, and a number of bankrupt companies which had manufactured products in similar or related fields. In 1993 Augustus Mill was purchased in Buckley Street. In 1971 the company purchased Macclesfield Private Preparatory School at 142 Chester Road to prevent

In 1969 Peter set up a Young Person's Christian Fellowship at his home, and he and his family have organised evangelistic holidays for young people every summer and Easter since 1971 at properties which he owns in Llanfairfechan, North Wales.

Peter has always made one thing very clear, namely that the only reason why the business exists at all or continues to exist is to enable the Christian evangelistic work to go on. Every year at the works Christmas Party he delivers a forty-five minute message on the meaning and the message of Christmas.

Martin, Stephen and Oliver Allmand-Smith, Peter's sons, share their father's faith and are all involved in the family firm. Jeremy, the second son, had also begun to learn the business when he was killed in a tragic motorbike accident in October 1981; this sad event was recorded in the family Bible alongside the births, marriages and deaths of everyone born into the Allmand-Smith/Watts family in the past 200 years. This Bible, dated 1772, can be seen in a photograph and which stands on Peter Allmand-Smith's desk, a constant source of strength and an ever-present symbol of the family's profound faith which is, and will remain, so central to all its undertakings.

Above: The current Board of Directors. From left to right: Peter Allmand-Smith (Chairman), Oliver Allmand-Smith (Managing Director), Martin Allmand-Smith (Marketing Director), Stephen Allmand-Smith (Finance Director). **Top left:** *The Regency Mill, standing since 1790.* **Facing page Bottom left:** *Some of Stormguard's wide range of products today.* **Facing page, bottom right:** *Stained glass panels are constructed by craftsmen in traditional designs.*

Looking good on paper

Nineteen ninety-nine sees the 70th anniversary of the founding of Slater Harrison - a remarkable Company today going from strength to strength at its home in Lowerhouse Mills, Bollington.

It was in the Depression-riven year of 1929 that Mr C F Leigh Slater and Mr J A Harrison first began trading as board pasters for hand-painted window bills and showcards - in direct competition with their former employers: Messrs Henry and Leigh Slater Ltd. Economic conditions had already proved catastrophic for many other local firms, but the duo were industrious and optimistic. To outsiders, nonetheless, their prospects must have looked decidedly dim.

The new Company was established at Ingersley Vale Mills. Formerly occupied by the Bleachers' Association and situated by a large pool in an idyllic corner of the undulating Cheshire countryside, the premises were let to Slater Harrison at an annual rent of £285. Plant at a cost of £2,500 was purchased and installed and production started in June 1929. In those days the firm concentrated on laminating paper to paper, and paper to board to create what was called pasteboard. Cloth-lined boards were also produced to supply the printing industry. From the outset an impressive array of densities, colours and finishes was available, attracting a ready stream of customers. Much of the work was hand pasted although a continuous pasting machine was pressed into operation for lighter substances. The paste used was flour-based and took up to 48 hours to dry thoroughly.

In May 1930 - in defiance of the continuing slump - Slater Harrison opened a sales office in Fleet Street, London. Development continued, albeit slowly, at a steady rate over the next few years. In 1933, however, the Company's engineers faced a significant challenge: Germany at the time was producing cheaper pasteboard which had begun to pose a threat in the British market - it became essential to discover some means by which production could be increased at Bollington, thereby reducing costs, so that existing customers would not be tempted away.

Their solution was the construction of a new machine and the

Above: The Chairman and Managing Director, Mr O C Dixon, OBE in the 1940s/50s.
Left: The founders Mr Slater and Mr Harrison in the 1930s.

adoption of a dextrine adhesive. Board manufactured in this way could be dried on the machine, drastically reducing production time and ensuring for the company renewed dominance in the market.

Rising mechanisation at the mill, however, made increased demands on electricity consumption. In 1932 Ingersley Vale's majestic water wheel took over the role of power generation. Thought then to be some 120 years old, it was the largest working water wheel in the country. Constructed on a giant cast iron shaft it measured 56 feet in diameter, and 10 feet 6 inches across its buckets. For five years it successfully drove the dynamo that supplied all the factory's electricity.

In 1935, Slater Harrison made a landmark decision: to diversify into paper coating as part of a major programme to expand its already extensive product range. Wide-ranging enquiries were made and the prevailing technology examined before an order was made for the necessary machinery in 1936. While it was being constructed, Lowerhouse Mills (a former cotton mill) came on the market, and was too good an opportunity to miss - space at Ingersley Vale was already under pressure and the new machine would make the situation almost intolerable. A price of £7,000 was agreed for the new premises and the move took place in stages over a number of months, with production only minimally disrupted. By December 1937, Slater Harrison was successfully installed in its spacious new home (with twice the floor area

previously enjoyed in Ingersley Vale), the paper coating machine came into commission, and a new era dawned.

If Mr Harrison and Mr Slater devoted much of their energy to product development and capital investment, their workforce was not forgotten. Sons and daughters of staff first employed in the 1930s are preparing to celebrate the company's 70th birthday as employees themselves, many with a history of service that stretches back twenty or thirty years. This loyalty, all too rare in our day and age, has at its root the strong sense of community that Messrs Slater and Harrison were able

Above: The original company announcements, 1929 showing the Ingersley Vale Mills, Bollington.
Below: The finishing room where the boards were sorted.

under ideal weather conditions. The whole of the expenses of the outing were borne by the firm, and all the directors accompanied the party' (from 'The World Paper Trade Review' September 1937).

But the bright days were not to last. Mr Harrison's death in April 1939 presaged a sombre spell for the Company. When war broke out in September, the supply of materials was rapidly curtailed and the workforce steadily depleted. When paper rationing was announced, word spread through the industry that soon only licensed business would be permitted, and no quotas would be available for the small demands on which the firm depended. By the end of 1940, the writing seemed to be on the wall and the

to inculcate in the early days. Every member of the workforce was valued for his or her particular contribution and a close-knit family atmosphere became the norm. In the 1930s there were regular social events, including a popular annual outing to Llandudno when the entire staff took private coaches on a train to Liverpool, boarded the SS 'St Tudno', sailed to Llandudno where they 'followed their own inclinations for the afternoon. The return journey from Llandudno was made by boat at 5pm for Liverpool, tea being served on board. The sea trip was rendered particularly pleasant by reason of brilliant sunshine, tempered by a fresh breeze. Bollington was reached again at 11.30pm, after a thoroughly enjoyable day

Above left: Executives smiling for the camera before doing their paperwork in the 1930s.
Above right: Staff hard at work in the factory.
Below: Staff having barrels of fun in the Colour Shop.

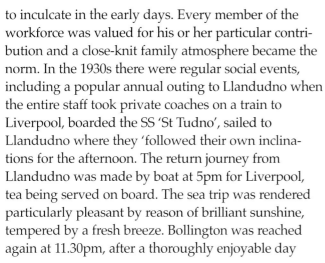

Directors reluctantly agreed that the works should be shut down for the duration of the war. An anxious workforce were served their notice - and a cloud of unprecedented pessimism descended on Lowerhouse Mills.

A chance encounter, however, changed everything. Slater Harrison's representative in Liverpool, a Mr Rider, happened to mention the Company's imminent closure to Mr H L Dixon of L S Dixon & Co Ltd. Mr Dixon was immediately interested. His own company, a large paper merchants, had lost both its factory and its offices during successive blitzes on the city - and he was keen to find replacements. Talks with Slater

Harrison were fruitful and in December 1941, L S Dixon & Co purchased the firm for £10,500. The name of the company was changed to Slater Harrison & Co (Bollington) Ltd, the mill welcomed a new manager in the form of Mr F G Bannister, and there was a collective sigh of relief all round.

As the war progressed, Mr Bannister was able to ascertain that a limited quota of essential materials could indeed be obtained for the service of small orders. Licensed business, as much as the firm could attract, provided the mainstay of its wartime work but

Above: The coating machine in the 1960s.

the resumption of small orders did much to re-establish its commercial base. When peace arrived in 1945, demand increased so rapidly that it was soon outstripping supply; the Company quickly responded by installing more machinery. In 1947 a second coating machine was commissioned, and a House of Dixon Newsletter memorably recorded the mood of the time at Slater Harrison:

'Their works are always a flurry of activity, and their staff is nearly up to full strength again, and many have rejoined from the services. In this connection a point of interest is that the 'El Alamein' Anniversary Reunion programmes were printed on one of their two-sided Art Boards, and were the subject of much favourable comment by the 'high-ups' present...Wives would be green with envy if they saw the meals that are provided by the Canteen - now very much a going concern - supplying nearly 90 lunches a day at less than one shilling (5p) per head.'

So it was that a period of sustained growth - sustained by an atmosphere of postwar optimism - began in earnest.

By 1957, a new floor of offices was added, which later incorporated the firm's laboratory and the canteen. In 1959, the company reverted to its old name of Slater Harrison & Co and in 1960 bought its premises back from L S Dixon for £35,000 (retaining them until they were sold again to the L S Dixon Group in 1971 for £51,913).

In 1960, the firm acquired its first company-owned lorry - a 7 ton Austin diesel, costing £1,600. In the same year, an impregnating machine was installed and the firm saw industrial paper production for the first time. A series of experiments and a programme of practical development led in 1961 to the first manufacture of the internationally known Day-Glo fluorescent paper and board - an area which still sees Slater Harrison as market leader - and confirmed a reputation for innovative ideas and applications which has stood the Company in good stead ever since.

By 1965, a new stock shed was in operation, and the programme of expansion at its height. In 1967, the registered capital of the Company had risen to £200,000 (from an initial investment of £5,000), and the future seemed secure.

Characteristically, the economic downturn of the 1970s was greeted by the firm as a moment of opportunity rather than of misfortune. Under Mr M D Harrison's astute guidance as Managing Director, the Company's laminating operation was streamlined and modernised. At the same time, the Company was rewarded by a stroke of luck: one of Slater Harrison's chief competitors in Ticket Boards - Henry & Leigh Slater Ltd - decided to discontinue their production of

Above: Impregnating machine in operation.
Left: Representatives and members of staff in 1959 outside the company premises.

boards and offered Slater Harrison their laminating machine, and their goodwill, for £35,000. Still more expansion proved necessary, just as other businesses were being driven to the wall, when Henry & Leigh Slater's customers switched enthusiastically to Slater Harrison for their laminated boards.

As Slater Harrison look towards their 70th anniversary they can be proud of their undoubted achievements in the past and their continuing success today. From the outset, and encouraged by those early small-scale orders for individual customers, they have established an enviable reputation for responding quickly with tailor made solutions. Technical staff at Lowerhouse Mills have grown particularly adept at producing innovative ideas to meet a spectrum of challenges. In more recent years, a number of new products have seen the light of day. Coated ink-jet papers hold particular promise for the future. Unlike nearly every other manufacturer, Slater Harrison can produce both white and coloured ink-jet papers - the range even runs to Day-Glo colours - which gives them a unique position at the head of a huge market. Ink-jet printers can now generate photographic-quality images, and home-produced posters and graphics offer tremendous appeal for the pc user. Another innovation has been pre-pasted wallpaper - the process involves applying a hot starch coating to the paper - for a leading wallpaper manufacturer.

Another significant development dates from the early 1980s when a paper agent approached the firm with an idea which was enthusiastically taken up - furniture lamination. In this process, the same paper used in the production of flat panels is employed to convert foil into a bonded two or three ply impregnated laminate which can then be applied to the edges or mouldings of furniture - where it is impos-

sible to stick the foil directly on to the chipboard, because the uneven texture would be felt through the foil. This revolutionary process now accounts for a significant portion of Slater Harrison's business and has generated an entirely new department of its own. Next time you take a trip round a furniture store, look closely at the bedroom, lounge and dining furniture - all benefit these days from Slater Harrison's versatile laminates.

Led by Colourmount, mountboard for picture framing, which was also introduced in the early 1980s and is now becoming a market leader, the current product range is astonishingly wide and constantly expanding. Recent innovations include a technique to coat leatherette paper for gift boxes, and fluorescent photocopy paper marketed under the abidingly successful Day-Glo name.

Underpinning Slater Harrison's unimpeachable reputation is a commitment to quality. Standards are constantly examined and the manufacturing process is characterised by regular inspection at all stages - from raw materials to finished product. Quality of service is regarded as equally important. Most stock lines are delivered to customers within two or three days, many faster, and even tailor made solutions - for which the Company is still renowned - can be produced within 24 hours, provided that the raw materials are available.

Seventy years is a long time in business. Slater Harrison has flourished across the decades thanks to a coherent ethos that embraces opportunity, welcomes technical challenge, relishes the demands of quality and good service, and - perhaps most of all - recognises that the wellspring of success comes from the 120 strong workforce who today constitute the business, and community, of Slater Harrison & Co Ltd.

Above: An aerial view of the company in 1993.
Below: A close up view of the company.

BWT - Flying high and riding the thermals

James William Baxter was a man who knew an opportunity when he saw one. The year was 1836; King William IV was on the throne, the cotton trade was booming and Manchester was beginning to establish itself across the world as the centre of the textile industry. Cotton, therefore, was James Baxter's wise choice when he decided to set up in business as a 'manufacturers' merchant', dealing in cotton goods.

The fledgling company, destined within 50 years to become Baxter, Woodhouse & Taylor, grew and thrived despite the 'cotton famine' caused by a blockade of southern US ports during the American Civil War. By 1843 James' son Frederick was working alongside him in the firm, and it was not long before the expanding business called for a move. Father and son acquired a large warehouse in George Street, where the facilities included a hydraulic lift, gas lighting and four floors of space. A telephone was installed in 1877, and Baxters, one of the earliest firms in Manchester to have a telephone, took the number 294. In 1871 there was a further development when the company acquired the trade name 'Falconia', with a falcon logo and the Latin inscription 'Virtute non Verbis' (by virtue not by words).

It was on James William's retirement in 1887 that his brother Frederick became Managing Director; Robert Woodhouse, who invested capital in the business, was appointed a director, and John Crawshaw Taylor was appointed as Secretary of the firm. When Fred Baxter retired Mr Taylor became MD. The company subsequently began trading as Baxter Woodhouse & Taylor.

By the turn of the century the company recorded a profit of more than £1,7672, and was even then making its presence felt elsewhere, with a London office and agents established abroad. In response to further growth, in 1906 a second move was made to 24 Mosley Street, where the company occupied a large warehouse and extensive office space.

Above: BWT products in the late 1940s at a textile show.
Left: The original headquarters in Manchester.

himself unpopular with the rest of the workforce by using the clean table used for material to lay out his oily wire, which he then proceeded to cut up with the cloth shears. Woven wire mesh, adhesive zinc oxide tape, copper gauze, rivets and heavy-duty press studs formed part of Eric's experimentation, and a couple of weeks later he produced his very first heated suit, socks and gloves: Windak electro thermal flying suits had been born.

The new suits were eagerly adopted by the Air Ministry, and crews in unheated bombers and fighter planes had reason to be very thankful for Eric's invention during the long cold flights they made in World War II. After the war, Eric Taylor gained a special award for his valuable invention.

The company was honoured by a royal commission when they were asked to make a heated jacket for King George VI, who suffered chest problems (and eventually died from cancer of the lung). The King was able to travel in comfort by plugging the jacket into his car's battery.

The years of the Great War were difficult ones; between 1914 and 1918 exports declined, and in addition the company missed the input of two of its directors, Fred and Ernest Taylor, who both signed up for military service. The firm survived, however, and moved in 1920 to George Street where BWT remained for nine years. On their move to Sackville Street in 1929 the building in George Street was demolished and the site used for a cinema. Profits from the sale saw the company through the hard times of worldwide depression.

In 1932 BWT were granted the sole rights to sell a new showerproof gaberdine fabric. Eric Taylor, Fred's son, was responsible for the firm's specialised fabrics, and the potential of this wind- and rain-proof fabric was quickly spotted by the innovative young man. Developing his new ideas, Eric designed special garments and equipment for Arctic and Everest expeditions. Taking the concept a stage further he began to experiment with electrical elements in his own home workshop. One day he arrived at the warehouse and immediately made

The war years were significant for the firm, as during the December blitz of 1940 fire swept through the warehouse, totally destroying the building. The employees were all found temporary jobs in other areas. In 1941, after maintaining a position in Manchester city centre for more than a hundred years, BWT moved out to a silk mill in Poynton that had surplus space available on the first floor. The company eventually took over the entire building, and stayed there until 1947 when further space was needed for the development of new products. Another move followed, to an older building, also in Poynton, and an additional warehouse was also opened in Manchester, where specialised fabrics and grey cloth (natural, undyed materials) were handled. Fibreglass materials were handled at the Poynton premises.

Above: Pressurised flying suit, produced by BWT. It was demonstrated by one of the employees to show the flexibility of the suit in the late 1960s.

knitted and woven nylon, polyester, terylene and viscose were developed and were increasingly used instead of natural fibres. Determined to keep abreast of innovations, BWT developed new materials and technology that responded to the needs of industry - especially in the fields of diving and aerospace. Gradually, the aerospace business grew to form a significant proportion of the company's sales. In the early 1960s Eric Taylor designed a pressure suit for use in outer space, and though the suits were never put into production they were used in a commercial feature film 'The First Men in the Moon'. Every employee was invited to a special screening of the film at the Paramount Cinema in Manchester, and given a copy of the souvenir programme.

Soon after this, North Sea oil exploration led to a shift in emphasis from outer to inner space, and Baxters began to develop deep diving suits for an offshore diving company. Ministry contracts for breathing apparatus and electrically heated clothing to be worn under dry suits followed.

Over the years Baxters handled a wide range of products; during the 1920s they had specialised in cloth linings that had a multitude of uses, from shoe and hat linings to overcoats and camera bellows. Later they began to produce low-voltage electric blankets which they continued to produce until 1979. Heated foot muffs proved useful to London Zoo to transport snakes, and other similar developments included wrap-around bandages for sick monkeys and other small animals, heated pads for horses' legs and knees, and even a large heated blanket for elephants! The 1950s also saw an increasing involvement in insulation and other aircraft products.

Lightweight shower-resistant poplin was developed, and proved popular for children's jackets and trousers; ski jackets and the first anoraks were manufactured.

Nationwide, the 1960s and 70s were years of scientific development and progress. Man-made fibres such as

Above: BWT early pressure suit.
Right: Monty's jacket made from material supplied by BWT.

Acoustic and thermal products for the aircraft industry, a field where weight and compact design are crucial considerations, continued to be developed; insulation, de-icing devices, lightweight tubing and side-wall ducting were produced, and major orders came in for ducting for the VC10 and the BAC1-11 aircraft. Fibreglass canopies for the cockpit roof of Trident aircraft, louvre ducting for passenger planes, tubing for 'Concord', PVC-coated

nylon ducting for the 'Viscount' and 'Vanguard' aircraft, electrically-heated carpet underlay for the 'Comet' - all have come within the company's scope of specialist products. In 1992 the firm received the Queen's Award for Export, setting the seal of royal approval on the company.

Baxters' strong tradition for being a family-run firm continued until the mid 1990s, when BWT became part of Cork Industries Ltd, a group of specialist engineering companies based in the UK - a move that provided the company with the resources to implement further developments. A major programme of investment ensured further important research into product design and process, placing BWT in a strong position of expansion in the market place.

Today BWT is recognised as a world leader in the design and manufacture of ultra lightweight low pressure air distribution and insulation systems, establishing itself as a preferred supplier to the aerospace industry worldwide.

It is BWT's dedicated engineering team that is responsible for every process that takes place, and computer aided design makes it possible for them to visualise a product at every stage of its development, from the conception of a design right through to production.

Maintaining the highest standard of reliability and quality has long been at the head of BWT's priority list - even during the 1920s every piece of cloth was closely examined - and the company's quality management team ensures their compliance with both the civil and military quality assurance

requirements, providing a constant input throughout the entire manufacturing process.

The company's traditional commitment to customer support has contributed largely to their success.

On-site support is given at the clients' own premises during the process of design and final installation. BWT also provide day-to-day support, and a member of the firm's Customer Services Team provides a vital point of contact for each client.

The successful company that grew from a small cloth merchant more than 160 years ago looks set to continue to prosper into the next millennium, and eagerly looks forward to the further opportunities and challenges that the future years will bring.

*Above: Richard Branson promoting BWT's products in the 1990s. He also signed the photograph. **Left:** BWT products today.*

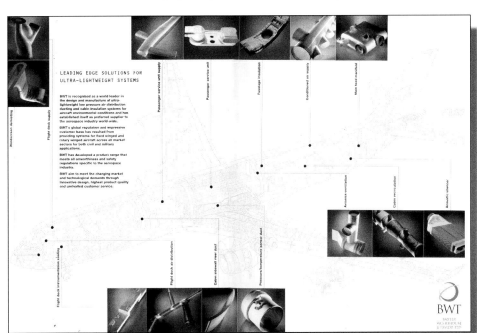

The company founder who was quick to see the light - and make a bowl to fit it

The invention of plastic almost 50 years ago revolutionised the manufacturing industry, presenting the consumer with a whole new range of products, and the manufacturer with a whole new range of challenges. John MacDonald, an ex-RAF engineer, was quick to see the opportunities and equally quick to seize his chance and find a niche in the marketplace which was about to open up. On returning to civilian life he had been employed by a company which manufactured cardboard boxes; this company had looked into using plastic as an alternative material, and John MacDonald had been part of the team who undertook the study. When the company took the decision not to proceed, he was reluctant to lose the opportunity to be at the forefront of developments. Realising that many, many items would be made out of plastic just as soon as the equipment with which to manufacture them was developed, John MacDonald went one step further, and, rather than sit and wait for someone else to make the machinery, he built his own vacuum former machine. Created at the very start of the plastic industry, this was probably the very first vacuum former machine ever built. With this machine he set to work in his garage at home in Wilmslow, and in 1959 a dedicated vacuum forming facility was established.

In a small industrial unit in Alderley Edge, the company concentrated on the manufacture of replacement lamp bowls for roadside and amenity lighting, with customers drawn primarily from the highways departments of various local authorities and their lighting contractors. In more recent years the company has diversified and can now offer to those same clients a wide range of complementary roadside mouldings and fabrications, including roadside

column mountings and period fittings, made from high impact acrylic and polycarbonate materials.

> "RATHER THAN SIT AND WAIT FOR SOMEONE ELSE TO MAKE THE MACHINERY, HE BUILT HIS OWN VACUUM FORMER MACHINE"

Many of the street-lighting items which the company makes are stock items to replace damaged parts, but special items can also be manufactured to order. Besides street furniture, Vacuum Formers Limited produces a wide range of general purpose industrial mouldings; it makes transit trays for the pharmaceutical industry, and for the computer industry it supplies keyboard trays for assembly. The company uses acrylic and polycarbonate materials, ABS, PETG, polythene, polystyrene and polypropylene, and has full manufacturing capabilities to work to any thickness from 0.5mm to 6.0mm. It has eight machines, of which six were built by John MacDonald himself, so there is nobody better qualified than John to know exactly what the machines can do. Vacuum Formers offers a complete in-house development service, with a dedicated team of highly trained and experienced design engineers on hand to assist customers set their product specifications. It is in this area where Vacuum Formers Limited has a real advantage over its competitors, because it is competent to handle all stages of product development, from concept drawings to full production; any technical problems encountered at any stage can quickly be solved by the combined experience and skills of the team. Their experience also enables them to assess the complexity of the processes involved and thus forecast accurately the lead times for prototype productions, which is invaluable to their clients as it permits them to fix realistic production schedules.

Not counting John MacDonald's garage, Vacuum Formers has moved premises three times: first to

Alderley Edge, then to London Road, Macclesfield, and finally in 1972 to its current premises at Brunswick Mill, Pickford Street, Macclesfield. It was at this site that the company was hit by a fire in the early 80s; the production department was destroyed by the blaze, but the business was able to recover and was soon back on the road to prosperity.

The second generation of MacDonalds is now involved in the company: John's son Andy, who has been involved in the business for 20 years, is now Director, and supported by Works Manager Ged Lashford. John MacDonald is semi-retired but still plays an active role. Although Vacuum Formers Ltd has moved a long way from the garage in Wilmslow where John's idea first began to take shape, the motivation of the company has remained the same: to respond quickly to the present and future needs of its clients, and to maximise the potential of each advance in the field of materials technology. Plans for the foreseeable future include major investment in semi-automated machinery which will increase the factory's cost-effectiveness and so help to ensure that Vacuum Formers Ltd retains its position at the forefront of its own specialised field; but what makes this company truly exceptional is the experience and dedication of its team, inspired by the man who pioneered the machinery and techniques which are still in use today.

Below: A nostalgic aerial view of Brunswick Mill around the 1960s, where the business began and will continue to prosper through the next millennium.

A dedication of time put into a prospering business venture

It was in a dilapidated two-up two-down rented cottage in a small yard off Stanley Street that welder and blacksmith Eric Burgess started to take on work for friends and family during the evenings after work and at weekends. Eric had served his apprenticeship at Watt's foundry in Catherine Street and was now eager to improve his fortunes and go into business on his own. As the number of orders for his services increased he was able to give up his job and dedicate all his time to the new venture.

A wide variety of work came his way: repairing broken machinery and tools for local farmers, manufacturing hand-forged wrought iron gates, standard lamps and coffee tables, repairing car body work - even fixing runners to children's sledges during the winter. He also produced sledges which were sold through Bayleys Toy Stores. Outside work also came to him from local firms such as Ray's mineral waters, Barrack's fabrics and Chelford cold store.

For the first few years the entire Burgess family were involved in establishing the business. Eric's father Joseph Burgess was responsible for the book keeping, while his wife Ethel and daughter Jean rolled up their sleeves and pitched in during the evenings, helping in any way they could from brewing pots of tea to welding and drilling. Brother Kenneth became a full-time employee and

eventually Ken's wife Kathleen took on the responsibility for all the office work.

The 1950s saw the expansion of the business, and a couple of run-down garages on the opposite side of the yard were rented and the necessary blacksmith's forge and anvil were set up. A new workshop was built for the lathes, drills and other equipment.

It was during that same decade that the company developed the important device which became known as the 'Goddard Gard Stick'. Produced for use in domestic sinks, the disinfectant stick was inserted

Above: Eric and Ethel Burgess in 1963. The founder of the business.
Left: Eric Burgess with his brother Ken with the guard stick at the original premises in Stanley Street.

into the plug hole where it collected waste and disinfected at the same time.

The product was sold to Goddards and became very well known across the country.

E R Burgess made a further move in 1964 to Brunswick Works in Lowe Street, an old silk mill which had been built around the turn of the century, a move which was made financially possible by the sale to Goddards of the Gard Stick.

The 1970s saw a change of emphasis within the company when the Hovis mill closed down.

E R Burgess took over the production of the bakery tins - and took on a number of Hovis' staff. Today the manufacture of catering utensils and equipment for bakeries in Britain and abroad has become their main interest, general engineering (which includes the use of gear cutters, saws, surface grinding equipment, brake presses, guillotines and hole punching equipment) only forms around 30 percent of the company's turnover.

A family firm in the true sense of the word, four generations of the Burgess family have been involved in the business. In the 1970s and 1980s Eric's two grandsons Christopher and Jonathan Sutton served their apprenticeships in the business. Jonathan is today the Company Secretary / Director and Jim Liptrot is Managing Director. Daughter Jean is now Company Chairperson.

Jonathan Sutton puts the success of E R Burgess down to the excellent quality of their products, their regard for customer satisfaction - and the firm's reputation for flexibility.

And their aim for the future? To develop new products, install innovative new machinery that will improve their output still further, and to go forward maintaining the high standard of service and quality for which E R Burgess has become known.

Above: From left to right are Jonathan Sutton, Jean Sutton and Jim Liptrot.
Left: Some of the products that the company produces today.

The Journeymen joiners who found the road to success

As the two Macclesfield-born joiners who, in 1894, set up in business in the building trade as Gorton & Wilson were to discover, making a new venture succeed can involve a tremendous amount of hard work and determination. The pair were skilled joiners, and their services were often called upon by outlying farms who wanted work done on their outbuildings. 'Papa' Gorton and George Wilson spent many an hour travelling over the sometimes long distances between one job and the next, pushing their tools with them in a handcart, and it was not unknown for them to spend the night in the barn they were working on rather than trek all the way home, only to come back again the next day. As a result of all their hard work during their first year in business together, the annual turnover was £500, the wage bill was around £85, and the balance sheet showed a trading profit of £14 0s 9d. In 1895, of course, these sums represented considerably more than they do today, and it was a sufficiently positive result to encourage Mr Gorton and Mr Wilson to persevere.

Within a decade or so, the firm of Gorton & Wilson had changed almost beyond recognition. 'Papa'

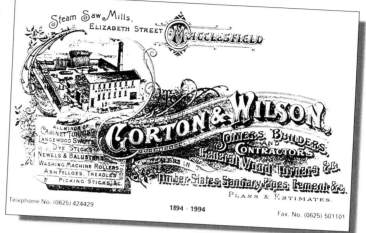

Gorton was no longer there, and George Wilson's son James had come into the business. James, who is remembered as a handsome, cigar-smoking young man, had inherited his father's determination and tenacity, and under his management Gorton & Wilson began to take on more purpose building contracts. Amongst the buildings which they erected during this period are the Majestic Picture House, the Church House at Buglawton, The Flowerpot on Congleton Road, some elegant properties on Ivy Lane, and a number of commercial premises including the water treatment plant at Langley. Edifices on this scale are quite a contrast to the washing machine rollers, treadles, dye sticks and picking sticks which were advertised on their elegant letterhead logo, and testify to the company's tremendous versatility. The firm's joinery skills found another outlet during the First World War, when it supplied a large quantity of wooden coffins to France.

The time was approaching when the third generation of

Above: A letterhead with the original factory which was demolished to make way for a motorway bypass. The company's other premises are still in Elizabeth Street.
Left: From left to right are Marjorie Wilson, Anne Barton, Sarah Kemp and Jonathan Kemp the current Managing Director.

Wilsons would join the family business. James's son Bert joined his father as soon as he left the King's School in 1922 at the age of 16, and was to work there and later run the business until he died in 1987, at the age of 80. During this time the firm's original factory, at the Steam Saw Mills in Elizabeth Street, was demolished to make way for the new bypass, and new premises were found nearby.

Bert Wilson left the company in the hands of his wife Margery and their daughter Anne, and since then the fifth generation of Wilsons has come into the business as well. Bert's daughter Anne Barton and his grand-daughter Sarah Kemp are now co-directors, and Sarah's husband Jonathan Kemp is Managing Director, in charge of the design and day-to-day running of the business. With less emphasis being placed on building contracts, Gorton & Wilson's main activities at present are hand-made fitted kitchens and bedrooms as well as building maintenance and traditional joinery. Traditional Design is a company set up within Gorton & Wilson Ltd, reflecting the change in emphasis of the business.

The fitted kitchen market has become very competitive in recent years. Gorton & Wilson as Traditional Design specialise in contemporary and traditional-style high quality, hand-made fitted kitchens designed and made by their own staff at the Elizabeth Street workshop. They will supply kitchens to any style or budget to meet their customers' requirements. They are also the local distributors for a wide range of kitchen appliances, moulding top brands seen as SMEG & BOSCH, which they are able to offer at discounted prices.

There will always be a place for traditional woodworking crafts, even though the days of washing machine rollers and treadles are long gone, and one specialised area where the firm's old-style craftsmanship is proving highly sought-after is in the construction of church furniture including pulpits, lecterns and pews.

Having discovered in its very early days that success does not come about without hard work, the company continues to do its utmost to provide the best possible service. In today's competitive environment, it recognises the importance combining a rapid response with high quality goods in order to attract and keep new customers; to this end, a new showroom which has been built at the new premises displays a range of the company's products. And founder George Wilson seems to have passed on his sound business sense as well as his enthusiasm and determination to each successive generation; future growth will be firmly based on the company's proven strengths, and the family will ensure that the venture continues to provide the quality service which generations of customers in Macclesfield have come to expect.

Top: One of Gorton & Wilson's extensive range of traditional English oak, free-standing sink units.
Above: The Gorton & Wilson story told in a local newspaper in January 1994.